LEARNING
RITUAL
MAGIC

LEARNING RITUAL MAGIC

FUNDAMENTAL THEORY AND PRACTICE FOR THE SOLITARY APPRENTICE

JOHN MICHAEL GREER, EARL KING, JR.,
AND CLARE VAUGHN

WEISER BOOKS
San Francisco, CA / Newburyport, MA

First published in 2004 by
Red Wheel/Weiser, LLC
With offices at:
665 Third Street, Suite 400
San Francisco, CA 94107
www.redwheelweiser.com

Library of Congress Cataloging-in-Publication Data

Greer, John Michael.
    Learning ritual magic : fundamental theory and practice for the solitary
apprentice / John Michael Greer, Earl King, Jr., and Clare Vaughn.
        p. cm.
    Includes bibliographical references and index.
    ISBN 1-57863-318-4
    1. Hermetic Order of the Golden Dawn. 2. Magic. I. King, Earl, Jr. II.
Vaughn, Clare. III. Title.
    BF1623.R7G75 2004
    133.4'3—dc22   2004010587

Typeset in ITC Legacy Serif Book by Dutton & Sherman Design

Printed in the United States of America

10 9 8 7 6 5 4 3 2

CONTENTS

INTRODUCTION

The lessons that follow were originally compiled as an introductory course in high magic for members of an independent Hermetic magical order. That order, now known as the Companions of the Rose (COR), remains active, but its focus and curriculum have evolved a good deal since the days when the course was first written and new members now follow a different course of training. However, because the original course proved to be an effective introduction to the fundamentals of Hermetic magical theory and practice, the governing body of COR decided to present it to the wider occult community in the hope that other students of the mysteries may find it useful.

Those who look through the following pages expecting to see a collection of rituals or other relatively advanced forms of magical working—the usual contents of introductions to magic these days—may come away surprised. While many people today are interested in magic, most start out by learning and trying to perform magical rituals, rather than attending to the more fundamental exercises and disciplines that make ritual magic effective (or even possible) in the first place. The result is very much as if a collection of would-be musicians tried to perform a symphony without first learning how to play their instruments.

For this reason, the course presented here devotes relatively little space to ritual, and the ritual workings that are included are quite simple. More space is devoted to meditation—the most neglected of all magical disciplines in the occult community at present and one of the most essential—and still more to a set of exercises intended to develop the absolute fundamentals of magical attainment: the basic skills of imagination, will, memory, and self-knowledge.

The essentials of magical theory are also discussed in the lessons, but the material covered differs again from the usual approach. Rather than launching into the details of Qabalistic or Hermetic philosophy, the course presents a series of basic perspectives. The aim throughout is to help you understand what magical philosophy is about, what its aims and purposes are, and why it matters.

Each lesson and exercise builds on those before it and lays foundations for the work to come, so it's important that the entire course be done in order. A certain amount of repetition is unavoidable, since few skills in (or out of) magic can be learned in a single attempt.

In its original form, the course was meant to be completed in nine months. This is certainly possible and beneficial, but it does require a certain amount of self-discipline and the willingness to set aside about thirty minutes a day every day for magical practice. It also requires a willingness to deal with the sometimes daunting experience of intensive magical work, and with its impact on the often ramshackle structure of the ordinary self. A less intensive approach that stretches out each lesson over more than the two weeks originally allotted for it can certainly be done by those whose schedules are tight, or who for one reason or another prefer a less demanding course of studies.

For the benefit of readers who do not belong to a magical lodge, a ceremony of self-initiation is included at the end of the book (see appendix A), along with a bibliography of books recommended for further study.

LESSON I

FIRST STEPS IN HIGH MAGIC

This first lesson deals with many things that, on one level, are matters of practical routine, but which on another lay the groundwork for everything you will do while working on the course.

Like the tradition from which it derives, this course should be experienced, not merely read or studied. A large part of the material covered involves practical exercises. You must allow time for these. The work of the first few lessons can be done in a few minutes a day, but the main body of the course requires more; most students need around half an hour each day.

It is surprising, and even embarrassing, to see how many would-be magicians decide that so small an investment of time is an insuperable obstacle to their progress. Most people learning to play a musical instrument, by contrast, realize from the start that time spent in practice is an essential part of the learning process. Most people who take up a martial art understand that it will involve long hours spent in the *dojo*. Magic is precisely the same. What you get out of it can be measured by what you are willing to put into it—and time is the essential ingredient in successful magical training. Sudden attainment of magical powers you have not worked to achieve is a matter for fantasy novels, not authentic magic.

To do the exercises presented in this course, and to get as much as possible from them, you must provide yourself with certain things. First among these is a suitable place to practice. Many of the old books in this tradition assume that the student can go to great extremes in this regard. Fortunately, this isn't necessary, as disused castles and desert hermitages are in short supply nowadays. A private room, not too brightly lit, where you can be undisturbed for half an hour at a time is quite sufficient. It should have enough open floor space so you can walk in a circle without bumping into furniture.

You also need a chair with a straight back—a folding chair is suitable. Some other things can be obtained from the school-supplies section of the local drugstore: a ruler, a pair of compasses (the kind used in geometry classes with a pencil clipped to one side will do), a set of colored pencils (the more colors the better), and a blank book or notebook for your magical journal.

Two other things, however, may take a visit to an occult specialist bookstore. The first is any three of the books listed below. While this course is meant to guide you in your practices over the next nine months, and will provide you with a solid grounding in the techniques of Hermetic high magic, it does not cover all of the philosophy, theory, and lore you must learn to become a capable magician. It would take a library to do that, not a single book! Most magicians do end up collecting a fair-sized library of magical books, but this course does not require that. Instead, it requires that you read, and learn from, at least three other books in the tradition during the course of your studies, although you may buy more than three if you wish. The booklist includes:

- W. E. Butler, *The Magician: His Training and Work*
- Dion Fortune, *The Mystical Qabalah*
- William Gray, *The Ladder of Lights*
- John Michael Greer, *Paths of Wisdom*
- Gareth Knight, *A Practical Guide to Qabalistic Symbolism*
- Israel Regardie, *The Tree of Life*

Some of these books date from the early part of the 20th century and contain ideas and expressions that many people now find outdated or even offensive. The major texts of Western esotericism, however, were written over a period of about twenty-five centuries, and contain a very wide range of viewpoints and ways of thinking about the world. Learning to be tolerant of such differences in order to extract useful material from older sources is an essential skill of magical study, one you should strive to develop as soon as possible.

The second item required is an appropriate tarot deck—and "appropriate" here means one that uses the same symbolic patterns central to this course. For any other esoteric work you're doing use any deck you prefer, but for the purposes of the course, we ask you to use one of the following:

- The Rider-Waite deck
- The Universal Waite deck
- The Albano-Waite deck
- The Magickal Tarot
- The Thoth Tarot, designed by Aleister Crowley
- The Gareth Knight Tarot
- The Hermetic Tarot
- The Golden Dawn Tarot
- The Golden Dawn Ritual Tarot

The work in these lessons requires that you use a tarot deck with the symbolism appropriate to the tradition we teach, and the decks listed here contain the proper symbolism in the proper form.

If you already own one of these decks and are comfortable working with it, by all means do so. If not, the most important thing to do is to find and use whichever of these decks makes you the most comfortable. Go to an occult bookstore that offers sample decks for the customer to look at and handle. Examine the appropriate decks one by one and select the one you want to use. If you dislike all of them, choose the one you dislike the least. As you make your choice, keep in mind that, if at all possible, you should use the same deck throughout the course.

Once you have your cards, store them somewhere where they will stay clean, dry, and undisturbed. You can wrap them in a cloth, or keep them in a bag or box, but placing them in a bureau drawer full of soft clothing will do just as well. Don't allow others to handle your cards, and never lend them to anyone.

Next, familiarize yourself with the cards. Even if you've used your deck for years, do the following exercise and try to look at your cards with new eyes. Each day, set aside five to ten minutes to work with your deck. Look at each card in turn, going through the deck as you would leaf through a photo album. Take a moment to absorb the image on each card, and then go on to the next. Record the practice in your journal, including anything you may have noticed or learned. Don't go on to do divinations yet; that will come later. Simply look through your cards each day.

DRAWING THE TREE OF LIFE

If you have had any previous contact with the Western esoteric tradition, you have probably encountered the diagram of circles and lines known as the Tree of Life. The ten sephiroth (in Hebrew, the traditional language of Qabalah, this means "numerations," though they are often called "spheres") and the twenty-two paths of this diagram form a map or set of coordinates for the universe and the human soul—that is, in the traditional terms, of the macrocosm (great world) and microcosm (little world).

Those who have had little contact with esoteric thought may find this idea unfamiliar at first. Perhaps the easiest way to grasp the idea of macrocosm and microcosm is to treat the Tree as a map of the structure of consciousness, since, in one sense, we can say that consciousness, or the "sphere of sensation," is like a magic mirror that reflects the world. But there is also the deeper sense in which this is true, because consciousness is the stuff of both microcosm and macrocosm.

Those who have studied the subject in the past may recognize the diagram of the Tree of Life as one of the key borrowings from the Jewish esoteric and mystical tradition called Qabalah. Although this diagram and much lore associated with it was adapted outside the Jewish world during the Renaissance, it was not taken over because it was new and different, but because it was new and familiar: many of the concepts, images, and structures were already well known to non-Jewish esotericists. In fact, very similar maps of the structure of existence were already in use in eastern Asia by the time the Tree first became well known in Europe.

Today, the Tree of Life is used by a great many different schools and systems of magic; few, however, are aware of the geometric plan that underlies the diagram. This plan derives from ancient traditions of sacred geometry and mathematics central to Hermetic magic. The following exercise will help you explore this aspect of the tradition. To do it, you need paper, a ruler and compasses, and a pencil.

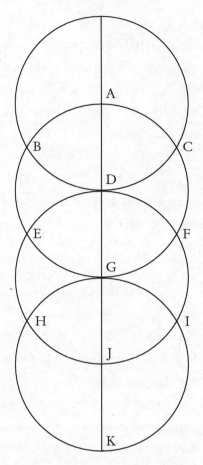

Figure 1. The sacred geometry of the Tree of Life.

1. Draw a vertical straight line on the paper (see the line ADGJK in figure 1 above).
2. With the compasses set at any convenient width, placing the sharp point near the top end of the line to locate the center, draw a semicircle (see line BDC in the figure).
3. Keeping the compasses at the same width, move the center to the point where the semicircle crosses the vertical line (at point

D in the figure), and draw a full circle around this point (circle ABEGFC in the figure).

4. Now repeat this operation twice, tracing each new circle around the point where the one before it crosses the central line (points G and J in the figure). Your diagram should now look like figure 1.

5. Set the compasses to a smaller width and trace a small circle around each point in the figure marked with a letter, except point D. These circles are the spheres, or sephiroth (numerations) of the Tree of Life (see figure 2, page 12).

If you wish, you can erase the larger circles and connect the sephiroth with paths, as shown in figure 2. For this lesson, however, this isn't necessary. The focus here is the geometrical relationship between the sephiroth and the process by which they are generated. These relationships and this process have an extensive symbolism and a wealth of meaning. For this lesson, however, simply work on drawing the Tree in this way a number of times (at least five) without trying to work up any conceptual or verbal interpretation.

EXERCISES

One of the things that sets the Hermetic tradition most sharply apart from mainstream Western religions, especially in their popular forms, is its insistence on practical work. In most faiths, it is enough merely to accept a set of propositions about the supernatural and perhaps follow some rules about how to behave. This rather simple (if not simple-minded) approach to the world beyond the realm of the senses probably has much to do with the popularity of these faiths, but it is not, ultimately, satisfactory.

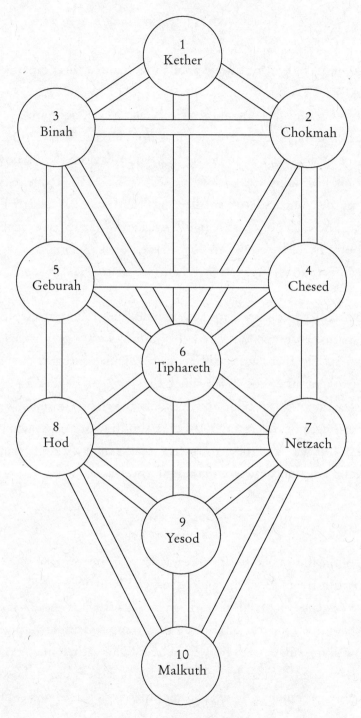

Figure 2. The Tree of Life.

is a skill, much as learning to deal with the world of meaning behind marks on paper is a skill. Few people who want to learn to ride a bicycle would be satisfied with a set of instructions that insisted that all they need do is lead a good life and believe in the existence of two-wheeled vehicles. Yet a very similar approach is taken by many people to issues that are among the most important any human being can encounter.

Ethical questions do have an important place in this work, and in lessons to come we will cover the main elements of the Hermetic approach to ethics. This does not involve learning lists of things to do and things not to do, however. Here, as elsewhere, the Hermetic approach takes as its basis personal experience and understanding. Our goal, when dealing with ethical issues, is to challenge you to learn what right and wrong mean to you—and then to put your discoveries to the test in your own life.

According to the Hermetic tradition, faith and a rule-keeping morality are not enough. Without personal experience of the hidden side of existence, in fact, they can be all but meaningless. Because of this, Hermetic magic (and this course) focuses mainly on ways to attain and assess such experience.

For this reason, we begin right away with practical work. By doing this work, you prepare yourself to deal more effectively with the theoretical aspects of the teaching presented in the lessons that follow.

You may be surprised to find that none of the practices in this lesson bear much resemblance to the ideas retailed by movies and fantasy fiction of what magicians do. Later in this course, the resemblance will be a little closer—but only a little! The main thrust here is to lay the foundations on which the more spectacular, and more widely publicized, methods of ritual magic depend. Too many novice magicians neglect these fundamentals, and then wonder why they are unsuccessful with more advanced methods of magical practice.

As suggested earlier, learning magic is like learning to play a musical instrument, speak a foreign language, or practice a martial art. The ease and grace of the advanced student is the product of steady, patient effort at more basic levels. Novice musicians must practice scales, language students must memorize grammar and vocabulary, and beginning martial artists must repeat basic forms and drills; there is no other way. In the same way, attention to the basics of magic now will pay off richly as you proceed further in your magical training.

A few notes about the practical side of these exercises may help here. It works best for most novice magicians to do exercises in the same place and at the same time each day; the habit thus established makes it easy to keep up with the requirements of the work. Privacy, quiet, subdued lighting, and clothes that do not bind or restrict your body are other useful aids to practice. Exercises involving relaxation, special patterns of breathing, or concentrated attention should not be done within an hour after eating a meal or making love; your energies have other things to do at such times.

OPENING AND CLOSING

One very simple, but very important, practice, the omission of which has caused quite a bit of trouble, is the use of opening and closing gestures. In this course, you will use a simple set of gestures that you can perform easily under most circumstances without drawing undue attention. Figure 3 (page 15) shows the steps of the opening gesture.

1. Begin with your hands placed together, palm to palm at about

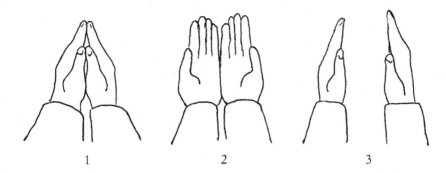

1 2 3

Figure 3. The opening gesture.

chest level, and held at an angle of about forty-five degrees.

2. Open your hands as though they were a book, with your palms facing you.
3. Separate your hands and turn them slightly so your palms are facing each other at a distance of about ten inches.
4. Move your gaze past your hands into the space between and beyond them.
5. Formulate the intention that your inner faculties are opening.

The closing gesture has the same steps, but in the reverse order.

1. Hold your hands apart, palm to palm.
2. Rotate them until both palms face you.
3. Bring your hands together, edge to edge, with your palms still facing you, as though you were supporting an open book.
4. Snap your hands together, as though you were snapping a book shut, with the firm intention of closing down your inner faculties.

This last movement has a percussive quality; if you can actually get your hands to clap, so much the better. The opening gesture should be performed at the beginning of each exercise; the closing at the end.

Relaxation

Systematic relaxation is widely taught today, and it is quite likely that you have already encountered it. It is a very useful skill to have, whether or not you have any esoteric interests. As with many skills, some mastery is better than none at all, but you can always improve your current level of skill. This lesson will make use of two methods. The first is common in occult circles.

1. Lie down on the floor or another flat, firm surface, and try to become as limp as possible. Unless you are already very good at relaxation, this is likely to be uncomfortable; the surface beneath you will show you precisely where your body is tense, and a host of previously unnoticed tensions will come to the surface of your awareness. Try to relax into them and let them pass off.
2. After a few moments, begin with one end or extremity of your body (your scalp or the fingers of one hand) and tighten one small segment of your musculature for a moment, until you are sure that it is in fact tight.
3. Release the tension.
4. Repeat this systematically throughout your whole body.
5. Go back and find the locations where tension has reemerged, and go through the whole process again.

It is rare that someone succeeds completely at this on the first try, so don't worry if you don't achieve complete relaxation at first. Give it a few minutes each day and you will find that the level of relaxation you reach will improve from day to day. Record the time and results of each performance of this exercise in your magical journal (see page 21).

The second method is rather different and is less common in occult circles today.

1. Sit in a comfortable, padded chair or lie down on your bed.
2. Draw in a deep breath, pushing out your stomach as you breathe in; you should feel the breath being pulled down to the bottom of your lungs.
3. Holding your breath, suck your stomach in, let it out, draw it in, let it out, draw it in, let it out.
4. Breathe out slowly, allowing your stomach to sink with the outgoing breath and relax completely.
5. Repeat the whole process three times.

Don't close your throat against the flow of air when doing this exercise. Unless you have very good breath control already, however, you're likely to find some of your breath escaping each time you suck in your stomach. The best way to overcome this is to keep on trying to draw in more air, while contracting your stomach muscles. You'll get the hang of it after some practice.

This second exercise helps teach relaxation and loosens and vitalizes the muscles and ligaments of the torso, where so many tensions are anchored. It also helps cleanse and energize the important subtle energy center at your solar plexus. Remember to use the opening and closing gestures at beginning and end of each exercise, and record the time and results of each practice in your magical journal (see page 21).

Attention

Although esoteric systems are notorious for their complexity, all their elaborate apparatus is, in an important sense, unnecessary or beside the point—ideally, at least. It is in the space between the ideal and the actual that the systems flourish; it is the general (though not universal) human inability to do things the simple and direct way that makes them necessary.

The following exercise is a concrete example of this. From one perspective, it is one of the basic "five-finger exercises" of the novice magician. From another perspective (some would say an impossibly optimistic one!), it is the only thing you need to know or do. All other means, exercises, teachings, and devices are for those who cannot do this exercise as it should be done.

In some ways, this exercise is the key to the development of the magical will. That description, however, can be either helpful or confusing, depending on how you think of "will." Esoterically understood, will is not exactly a matter of effortful striving; nor is the cultivation of will a matter of building up some distended, flaming, throbbing mental faculty that imposes itself on all and sundry like some big, overfamiliar dog. Developed will is effortless, simple, almost unconscious, and effective without needing a lot of fuss. The same thing is true of concentration. Effective concentration is not a matter of gripping something tightly, but of simply letting everything else go, as though you scooped up a handful of sand and rocks from the bottom of a stream and let the water carry away everything but the one pebble you wanted.

Do the following attention exercise at the same time every day, if possible, or at the same time in your daily cycle—for example, just after waking or just before dinner. At the beginning of your work on this lesson, don't do it for more than five minutes; by the end, you should be doing it for at least ten, but certainly not more than twenty, minutes at a time.

The exercise itself is simple. Stand, or sit, without moving throughout the exercise. Alternate standing and sitting: that is, on one day stand for the allotted time; on the next day, sit; on the next day, stand, and so on.

Before beginning the exercise, practice relaxation (see page 16), either as your main relaxation practice for the day, or as a brief "warm-up." When you are doing the exercise, don't try to do nothing, or think nothing, or feel nothing. At the same time, don't let yourself follow any thoughts or feelings that lead you away from being aware that you are sitting or standing (as the case may be). Instead, simply attend to the sensations of being in your physical body.

The usual position for seated meditation in this tradition, one you will use extensively later on, works well for this exercise as well. Sit in a straight-backed chair that allows you to have your feet flat on the floor, your thighs parallel to it, and your back straight. Place your hands on your thighs. For the standing posture, most people find it best to stand with their feet parallel and as far apart as their hips or shoulders. Experiment with different variations on these positions and pay attention to the changes that such variations bring about. The experimentation, though, does not count as part of the exercise time unless you do not move for the whole allotted time you are trying out that particular position.

At this point, don't worry about whether you are relaxed or tense. If you find uncomfortable or intrusive tensions, relax them if you can do so without changing position. Don't, however, try to maintain a rigid immobility. If nothing else, simply breathing will make your body move, and you may notice other movements as well.

Always try to bring your attention back to your body, without focusing on any particular part of it. Feel it as a unified whole, both in tactile and kinesthetic terms—that is, both through the sensations of touch on your skin and the inner awareness of musculature and posture within your body. Certain sensations may intrude. You may find yourself feeling discomfort, or restlessness, or itching, for example. Try not to flinch from these sensations, but attend to them calmly and easily, putting them in the context of all your other sensations.

Use the opening and closing gestures to begin and end this exercise, and record the times and results of the exercise in your magical journal.

DAILY RECOLLECTION

Every night before you fall asleep, think back over the events of the day in reverse, as though you were watching a film running backward. Start with the events that took place just before beginning the recollection, go to the events before those, and so on, back to what you did on waking up that morning. At this stage, don't try to judge or assess the things you remember. Just observe them. A reasonable amount of detail is appropriate, but the exercise should not take more than about fifteen minutes. If you fall asleep while doing the exercise, this is not a failure; your mind will continue to go back over the day's activities while you sleep.

This exercise has been put to exotic uses in some magical systems connected with the Hermetic tradition, but its basic point is more simple. Most people, according to one of the commonplaces of magic, go through life like sleepwalkers, paying little attention to their own actions and the events around them. Breaking out of this sleepwalker's trance is one of the purposes of magical training. In a very real sense, what makes magicians different from anyone else is that they are awake to the surrounding world and to the nature and consequences of their own actions. By learning to recall the events of each day in an unfamiliar order, novice magicians develop the ability to pay attention to their own lives; from this unfolds a range of unsuspected perceptions and abilities.

In your magical journal, note the approximate time at which you began this exercise, as well as how much of the day you reviewed before falling asleep.

The Magical Journal

Throughout this course, you'll keep a magical journal—a record of your esoteric training in which all of the practices and readings you do are noted. Include in each entry the date, time, circumstances, and results of your work, as well as any feelings or reactions you may have from doing it. Your magical journal will become an important resource for your training; make a habit of writing up each piece of work as soon as possible after doing it.

The specific format of the journal is up to you, but using a standard format makes it much easier to keep such a record. Here is an example.

12 June 1993

6:30 A.M.: Practiced opening and closing. Vague effect, nothing definite.

7:15 A.M.: Went through tarot deck after breakfast.

8:00 P.M.: Did the relaxation and attention exercises. Relaxation went fairly well. In the attention exercise, which I did standing, I wobbled all over the place and actually lost my balance at one point.

10:45 P.M.: Began review. Got as far as lunch, I think, then fell asleep.

LESSON REVIEW

1. Buy the necessary supplies (see page 6).
2. Begin examining the tarot deck (see page 7).
3. Become familiar with the process of drawing the Tree of Life (see page 8).
4. Perform the relaxation and attention exercises daily (see pages 16–18).
5. Perform the daily recollection on going to bed (see page 20).
6. Keep an account of your work in your magical journal.

When you have carried out the above exercises for at least two weeks, you are ready to proceed to lesson 2.

LESSON 2

THE UNIVERSE OF HIGH MAGIC

You have now had two weeks of experience with the most basic level of practices in Hermetic high magic, and with noting the way you respond to the discipline of regular practice. This discipline, and the self-knowledge and self-awareness that can be gained through it, have an important place in any system of magical work. Remember, just as it's impossible to master a musical instrument without developing the habit of regular practice, so the infinitely subtler instrument of human awareness can be mastered only through persistent effort.

At the beginning of this lesson's work, take some time to review your practice journal and assess the work you've done so far. Read through lesson 1 again and compare the way you did the exercises with the way they were presented. Try to gain some sense of the way in which you've been approaching the course. This should not be an exercise in passing judgment or self-criticism (or, for that matter, self-praise); nothing useful is gained from preening or punishing yourself. Simply review, assess, and determine if any changes in the way you handle the work are appropriate. This process—a sort of mid-course correction—should be done after each of the lessons of this course.

People differ; so do their reactions to the experience of taking up regular magical work. One pattern of reactions is relatively common, however, and worth discussing here. You may already have experienced something like it yourself.

In this pattern, the beginning stages of practical work seem interesting, even exciting; enthusiasm is easily come by and commitments, sometimes extreme, are easy to make. The work goes well, often surprisingly so.

After a certain point, however, the first rush of enthusiasm fades. Initial successes give way to frustration, fatigue, boredom. The commitments made so eagerly a short time before start to feel like annoyances, then hindrances, then intolerable burdens. Practices are postponed or forgotten, readings skimmed or neglected, and, fairly often, the whole process of practical work comes to a halt. Far too often, the pattern ends with the student, once so enthusiastic, dropping out entirely and either taking up something different or abandoning the idea of magical training altogether.

This pattern has many phases and many disguises, but a single source—fear. The human mind and personality often fear and resist change, particularly when that change puts at risk the carefully balanced fabric of compromises, inattentions, and little lies we use to cover the unacceptable aspects of our world and ourselves. By teaching the conscious use of the powers of human awareness, magical training opens up possibilities of growth and healing, but it also opens up self-knowledge—and this is by no means always a comfortable experience.

In many occult writings, this fear is symbolized by the somewhat florid image of the Watcher at the Threshold, a monstrous shadow-presence that must be overcome in order to pass the threshold of magical training. Aside from the real value of a name and a symbolism for this common experience, the image and lore of the Watcher has something of use to offer students of esoteric tradition. Like all legendary monsters, the Watcher has a chink in its armor, a secret vulnerability. If it is faced with simple persistence, it submits.

If you find yourself going through some form of the pattern described above—or, for that matter, if you are already in the middle of it—the one way out is to continue with the practices. Sometimes all that is necessary is a single effort of will, a decision to keep going despite the pressures to give up. Sometimes, a more extended effort is needed. Either way, the experience is itself a part of the process of training, and an important step toward the higher reaches of magical knowledge and power.

MAGICAL THEORY: LEVELS OF BEING

One of the central concepts of the Western esoteric tradition, and one of the major differences between that tradition and today's popular ideas about the universe, is that the universe exists, and can best be understood as existing, on many levels of being. Modern people tend to see the universe of matter and physical energy as the only reality, whether they consciously realize this or not. But from an older perspective, this is only one of several realms of existence. The relationship between these realms can be likened to that between the colors of the spectrum or the different frequencies of radio waves. They form a continuum between spirit and matter, or pure potentiality and complete manifestation.

This continuum of being can be illustrated using two interpenetrating triangles, as shown in figure 4 (see page 26). The unshaded triangle represents spirit, potentiality, or form, which are best understood as different ways of talking about the same thing. The shaded triangle represents matter, manifestation, or substance. Whatever terminology you use, keep in mind that these two triangles are not different things, but distinguishable states or modes of the same thing—the One Thing spoken of in alchemical texts, of which all other things are adaptations.

It is convenient, for practical purposes, to divide this continuum of being into several levels. The Four Worlds and ten sephiroth of Qabalistic theory, which you will learn about in your reading, can be used in this way. The Hermetic magical tradition contains several others as well. One very useful division involves marking out five levels of existence that correspond to five realms of human experience and thus to five realms of magical work. These, in turn, correspond to the five natural divisions shown in figure 4. These levels of being can be described as follows:

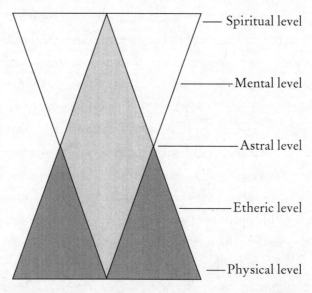

Figure 4. The interpenetrating triangles of the continuum of being.

Physical: The material world as perceived through the five ordinary senses. In Hermetic theory, the furthest outward extent of the process of creation, consisting of passive and formless substance, receiving its life and form through interactions with the higher levels of being.

Etheric: The subtle structuring energies that lie immediately behind the world of matter, corresponding to what yoga knows as *prana*, and the martial arts as *ki* or *ch'i*. Often apparently perceived through the ordinary senses, though actually perceived through their etheric counterparts. Many aspects of the body that seem at first to be properties of the physical body can better be ascribed to this energy body.

Astral: The realm of concrete consciousness, perceived by the imagination and, less directly, by other aspects of the mind. Most often, the level of ordinary human thought, and also the level of most magical workings. In the Hermetic tradition, the transmission fluid, so to speak, between matter and spirit.

Mental: The realm of abstract consciousness, containing the basic patterns or "forms" upon which creation is founded, perceived by the intuition and by the highest aspects of thought. A characteristic feature of this realm is its impersonality or trans-personality.

Spiritual: The realm of pure creative power emanating from the divine, beyond all definition or limitation. The highest mode of experience accessible to human beings, perceived only in the inmost core of the self.

This system will be used extensively in the following lessons, but it should not be taken as anything more than a convenient classification. Its one real advantage is that it provides a common language with which we can talk about, and point out, things that are otherwise hard to express. Please familiarize yourself with the terms and the way they are used here, and think about the ways that your own experience fits into these categories.

Though this course focuses on the scheme just given, the continuum of realms can be divided in other ways. For example, it can also be seen as ranging, not between form and substance, but between energy and form, each level being a reflection or inversion of the one before it. If the spiritual level is pure energy, the mental level is that energy coalescing into forms, and the astral level is the energies of those forms. This means that the etheric aspect of things is actually a mode of form, and that the material world is actually a mode of energy. This fits very well with the traditional idea that matter is, at root, an idea of limit or refusal, that its energy is one of resistance to the organizing forms. It also fits well with traditions that see matter as the sleeping place of a great energy that, when awakened, rises to the level of spirit to be the "mother of the king."

Another system of classification you will use extensively is based on the traditional concept of the magical elements. Many of us have heard that people once believed there were four elements: earth, air, fire, and water. This viewpoint is often associated with a certain amount of mockery, but, as with the mockery associated with the claim that people once believed that the Earth was flat (and that, by going too far, one could drop off the edge), the mockery says more about the limited knowledge of those who indulge in it than it does about what people actually once believed.

The four elements were not understood in the sense of the elements of modern chemistry and physics. They were not, in fact, originally a set of four, nor did they remain so. Among the early Greek philosophers, various substances were put forward at times as emblems of the basic substance of which everything was made. One philosopher proposed that water was the best emblem for the basic substance of existence; another proposed fire for the same role; yet others felt that the qualities of the world could not be reduced to any one basic quality, and so looked to some set of essential, irreducible qualities as the basic substrates that, in combination, represented the fundamental root matter of the world.

The final model, which dominated Western magic, science, and philosophy for almost 2,000 years, was originally proposed by the Greek philosopher and magician Empedocles in the fifth century B.C.E., and was put into its standard form by Aristotle about 150 years later. It includes the four elements—earth, water, fire, and air—and a fifth, known as the Quintessence (from the Latin for "fifth element"), or simply as spirit. This is the scheme you will use in this course.

The five elements are not static, unchanging counters. They are moments in a process of transformation, and the rules that govern the changes among the elements are important in every aspect of the Hermetic magical tradition. Each element can be seen as the result or product of two qualities. Thus, fire is hot and dry, while water is cold and wet. They are clearly opposites, and can be arranged as in figure 5 (see page 30), where fire appears at the top and water at the bottom. It is clear, then, that the two other elements are the products of cold and dry (at the left in the figure), and hot and wet (at the right in the figure), and that these qualities are traditionally ascribed to earth and air, respectively. The Quintessence is in the middle: it is the common substrate of all the elements. It is what remains constant as the elements transform one into another through changes in the balance of qualities.

The elements can also be arranged in a circle, as in figure 6 (see page 30). When the Quintessence is put at the center of the circle, there are many (in fact, twenty-four) ways to arrange the remaining

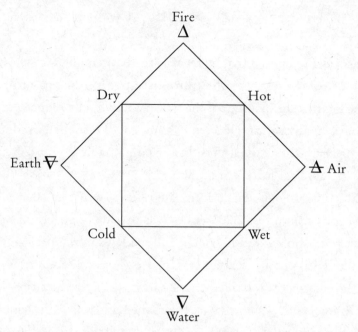

Figure 5. The four elements, their characteristics, and the Quintessence.

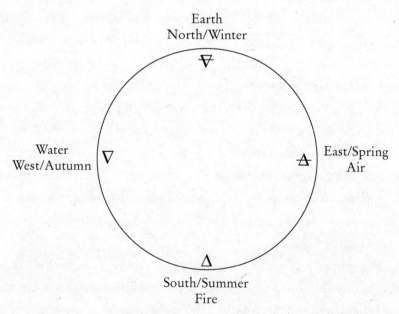

Figure 6. The four elements and the circle of the seasons.

four elements at the quarters of a circle. The arrangement in figure 6 links the elements with the seasons and directions: air with east and spring, fire with south and summer, water with west and autumn, and earth with north and winter.

The elements are also associated with the suits of the tarot deck: fire with Wands, water with Cups, air with Swords, and earth with the suit called in various decks Coins, Disks, or Pentacles. Finally, the five elements can also be arranged vertically and aligned with the five levels of being, as well as with the Qabalistic Tree of Life.

With this in mind, return to the process of drawing the Tree of Life learned in the last lesson (see page 8). This process, which generates four mutually defining curves along a central line, provides a clear graphic image of the emergence and interrelationships of the five elements. The central line corresponds to spirit, the Quintessence, and the four curves to the four elements. There is no fixed relation between a given curve and a given element; the circle of the elements can be drawn starting from any point and extended in any order.

Reading and Study

By this time, you should have purchased three books from the list included in lesson 1 (see page 7). These will form an important tool for training during the months to come. On one level, any of these books can be used as a source of useful information on Hermetic magic, in the same way that you might read books on auto repair or soap making to acquire background knowledge on the practical work of those crafts.

This sort of reading for general information, done quickly and often with minimal attention, is only a first approach to extracting the knowledge in magical texts, however. There is more to be had from most magical texts than this relatively shallow method can extract. In this course, a central goal is to introduce you to more effective ways to extract knowledge from magical texts. In the process, you will gain a mastery of methods that enable you to make sense of the entire literature of high magic, despite its habits of secrecy and evasive communication.

Choose one of your books and read the first chapter. Then go back through the same chapter with a pen and seven note cards or small pieces of paper and copy out, by hand, the seven sentences that seem to you to convey the most important ideas in the chapter. Take your time doing this; you may find it useful to write out a larger list, and then winnow it down until you have just seven sentences, one on each of seven note cards.

Keyboard fans will note that the final list of sentences should be copied in your own handwriting. This may seem unbearably old-fashioned, but the process of writing each sentence out by hand communicates it to the brain and the nervous system in a way that tapping it out on a keyboard will not. Magicians were once expected to write out their own books of magical practice, even when the same books could readily be had in printed form, for exactly this reason.

For each of the seven days that follow, make one of these sentences your faithful companion. Just before you start your daily recollection, take one of the cards, read the sentence on it, and think about what it means and what it suggests to you. Put the card in a place where you will see it when you first wake up the next morning. When you awaken, read it again; you may be too bleary to think much about it, but read it through. Put the card in a place where you will see it several times during the day, and each time you see it, stop, read it, and think about it. When you are caught in one of the time-wasting exercises that make up so much of modern life—waiting for a bus, standing in line, or stuck in traffic—call the sentence to mind and think about it.

When you get to the end of the day, set that sentence aside, choose another, and proceed as described. At the end of the week, go through the same process with the second chapter in your book, choosing seven sentences that express its most important ideas, and spending one day living with each of them.

In a later lesson, we'll talk about the point of this exercise. For the time being, simply enter into the experience and see what you learn from it. The sentences should be entered in your magical journal. If you wish to note down anything you figure out about them, by all means do so, but this isn't required.

Tarot: The Trumps

An important part of work with magical symbolism involves the cards of the tarot deck you have purchased. Over the years, an enormous amount of puffery and nonsense has been written about these cards. Claims of Egyptian or even Atlantean origins have been made on the basis of no evidence whatever; dozens of "original" versions have been designed and marketed; promises of vast powers and importance have been waved about. What lies behind all this clamor is a simple and useful collection of seventy-eight symbolic images that can be put to countless uses in magical study and practice.

While most people think of the Tarot as primarily a tool for divination—that is, predicting the future or obtaining hidden knowledge about the past or the present—this barely touches on the possibilities of the deck. The tarot is the Swiss Army knife of Hermetic high magic, and you can do almost anything with it once you know how. Learning how is one of the main purposes of this course.

You have now had two weeks to familiarize yourself with the deck you selected, and it is time to begin practical work. While there is a huge amount of lore on the meanings and correspondences of the cards' symbolism, this can be as much a burden as a help to the novice. For now, therefore, we ask you to approach the symbols and images of the tarot in a more straightforward fashion. Begin the first part of this lesson's exercise with these steps:

1. Deal out all the trumps—that is, the cards that do not belong to any of the four suits, and that are numbered 0 to 21, often in Roman numerals.
2. Put these cards in order by number, with 0 (the Fool) at the beginning and 21, or XXI (the World or Universe), at the end. The cards belonging to the four suits can be set aside for the time being, as they have no part in this exercise.
3. Go through the stack of trumps one at a time, looking at each of the images. Try to notice each of the symbols on each of the cards while you do this.
4. Lay out the trumps in order on a flat surface, so that they form a single line. This line forms a sequence or progression, and, in this sequence, symbols repeat themselves, sometimes in different forms.
5. Try to follow the flow of images and ideas from trump to trump. You may find it useful to think of the entire series of trumps as a story told in pictures, with the Fool as its central character. What seems to be happening in this story?
6. Spend as much time as seems useful doing this, then put the trumps away.
7. Be sure to write up your perceptions in your magical journal.

The second part of this lesson's practice is done at least two days later.

1. From your deck, draw out two of the trumps at random.
2. Set them down next to one another and examine them closely. What connections, similarities, or oppositions can you see between them?
3. Continue this exercise as long as seems useful, and write up your perceptions in your journal.

The first part of the exercise need only be done once during the two weeks you spend on this lesson; the second part should be repeated seven times, drawing a new pair of trumps each time.

CONSTRUCTING THE LITTLE WORLD

Much of the work you'll do in subsequent lessons focuses on the Tree of Life and its symbolism. As a tool to help you with this work, make a drawing of the Tree large enough to contain notes on the symbolism. As you fill it in, this diagram will truly become a *minutum mundum*, a miniature world that will be far more than a mere list of symbols and correspondences. This diagram must be completed and ready to use by the time you begin lesson 4.

1. Start with a large piece of heavy paper or tag board. Construct a Tree of Life using the method you learned in lesson 1 (see page 10). Make it big, but make it as exact as possible. Draw the constructing arcs lightly, since you'll need to erase them.
2. At each of the ten points on the diagram that mark the sephiroth, draw four nested circles as shown in figure 7.

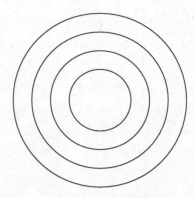

**Figure 7. Nested circles portraying the
Four Worlds of the Qabalah.**

(To draw these, set the point of the compass at 1/4, 1/2, 3/4, and 1 inch, respectively.) These will hold the symbols of the sephiroth in the Four Worlds of Qabalistic theory.

3. Draw the paths to match those on the Tree of Life shown in figure 2 (see page 12). They should be at least 1/4 inch wide, to allow you to write in the path symbolism.

4. To center the paths properly, draw a light guideline lined up on the centers of the two sephiroth that the path connects; then draw another line to each side of the guideline, parallel with it, say 1/8 of an inch away. The guideline can then be erased. All lines should end cleanly at the outer edge of each sephirah (the singular of sephiroth).

It may take several tries to make this diagram, but this should not be seen as a waste of time. The experience of constructing the Tree has lessons to teach that are well worth the time and effort involved.

Continue both of the relaxation exercises from lesson 1 (see pages 16–17) during the time you spend on lesson 2. As with all your practices, note down your practice sessions and experiences in your magical journal.

ATTEПTIOП: POSTVRE AПD BREATHIПG

For this lesson, continue with the attention exercise you practiced in lesson 1, (see page 18), but with the addition of rhythmic breathing. Sit in the traditional meditation position and, while you are sitting, breathe in a particular way—inhaling, holding your breath, exhaling, and again holding your breath before inhaling. Your periods of inhalation, exhalation, and stillness may all be equal (this is sometimes called "the fourfold breath," as each phase is done for a count of four), or your periods of inhalation and exhalation may be twice a long as your periods of stillness (thus 8-4-8-4). Pick one of these and stick with it for the duration of these lessons.

There are several points to remember in doing this. The first, and most important, is not to force yourself to maximum capacity or maximum compression. We are all so familiar with breathing that we take it for granted, but the sheer mechanical forces involved can actually cause damage if they are forced to extremes.

The second point is never to hold your throat closed during the phases of stillness. Stillness should come from stopping the movement of the muscles of the chest and abdomen (again, not by jamming them to extremes!), rather than by blocking the airway.

Third, do not rely on external timers such as metronomes. Try to rely on your own internal counting to establish the length of the phases. Ideally, time the phases by your pulse or heartbeat. Naturally, your pulse has no mechanical regularity, but achieving mechanical regularity is not the point. Learning to focus your attention is.

Breathe in and out through your nose, and use your abdomen as well as your diaphragm, filling and emptying your lungs as much as you can without strain.

Do the exercise for five to ten minutes at a time at the beginning of this lesson's work. Do not increase the time beyond twenty minutes during this lesson. Be sure to keep an account of this work in your magical record.

RITUAL: THE QABALISTIC CROSS

Ritual is one of the great tools of magic. The following, known as the Qabalistic Cross, is one of the "five-finger exercises" of magical ritual, yet it is also a ritual that, in and of itself, repays careful work and study. The Qabalistic Cross should be done once a day, if possible at the same time each day. It can be particularly useful at the end of your attention exercise each day, before you do the closing.

1. Stand facing east, feet together, arms at your sides. Visualize yourself expanding upward and outward into space, until the Earth can be seen like a sphere about a foot in diameter beneath your feet.
2. Raise your right hand above your head, then draw it down to your forehead. Visualize a beam of brilliant white light coming down from infinitely far above you to a point just above the top of your head, where it forms a sphere of white light, also about a foot across. Vibrate *Ateh* (pronounced "Aah-teh").
3. Draw your hand down to your solar plexus, and visualize the beam of light descending all the way down to the center of the Earth beneath your feet. Vibrate *Malkuth* (pronounced "Mahl- kooth").

4. Bring your hand up and across to your right shoulder, and visualize the light extending outward from the center of your chest to the right, forming one arm of a cross. Just beyond your shoulder, it forms another one-foot sphere, this time of brilliant red light. Vibrate *ve-Geburah* (pronounced "veh geh-boo-rah").

5. Bring your hand across to your left shoulder, and visualize the light following to form the other arm of the cross. Just beyond that shoulder, it again forms a one-foot sphere, this time of brilliant blue light. Vibrate *ve-Gedulah* (pronounced "veh geh-dyoo-lah").

6. Fold your hands across your chest, crossing at the wrists, right over left. Visualize the entire Cross shining with light. Vibrate *Le-Olam, Amen* (pronounced "leh oh-lahm, ah-men").

"Vibration" here refers to a special way of speaking or chanting words that infuses them with special qualities in magical ritual. To learn how to do it, find a tone that produces a vibrating or humming feeling in your body. This may not be especially loud—in fact, in most cases, it should not be. It's often best to experiment with a simple vowel sound such as "aaaaah" or "oooooh," playing with the tone, the position of your tongue, and the shape of your mouth, until you learn how to get the tone you need. With some practice, you may find that the buzzing or humming feeling can be localized at the spots touched by your right hand when doing this ritual.

The words themselves are a traditional passage from Jewish ritual that was also borrowed early on by the Christian church. *Ateh* means "unto Thee"; *Malkuth* is "kingdom"; *ve-Geburah* is "and the power"; *ve-Gedulah* is "and the glory"; *le-Olam* means both "throughout the world" and "throughout time." *Amen*, today little more than a bit of spoken punctuation at the end of conventional prayers, was once an important word of power; it means approximately "be it so."

LESSOΠ REVİEW

1. Perform the relaxation and attention exercises daily (see pages 16 and 18), along with the Qabalistic Cross (see page 38).
2. Perform the daily recollection on going to bed each night (see page 20).
3. Work with seven sentences from each of the first two chapters of a book from the list in lesson 1 (see page 7).
4. Do the Tarot Trump exercises (see page 33).
5. Build the Tree of Life as described above.
6. Keep a record of your work.

When you have carried out these exercises for at least two weeks, you are ready proceed to lesson 3.

LESSON 3

FOUNDATIONS OF
HIGH MAGIC

In this lesson, you will complete your introduction to the essential disciplines of magic. Each of the practices presented in these first three lessons is capable of expansion and development in many different directions, and we'll discuss many of the basic possibilities later. By the time you finish this lesson, however, you will have explored the core elements of the training program—and of the Hermetic magical tradition itself—in a very basic form.

These initial practices are central to all of the work of this course, as indeed they are to the teaching and practice of Hermetic high magic. Take the time to be sure you have a solid grasp of these methods before you go on. It is important in the first stages of practice to lay a good foundation, one that will not have to be taken apart and rebuilt later.

There is a wide range of traditional methods of magical practice. Some work well for nearly everyone, while others are effective for only a small percentage of people; most are entirely safe, though some can cause psychological or physical damage. Here, we introduce you to a set of basic techniques that are both effective and safe, in order to lay the groundwork for more advanced forms of magical practice.

Eventually, you can select your own methods from the treasury of Western magical traditions. For the time being, however, we suggest that you work steadily with the specific exercises we present and not mix them with others. Some combinations of practices tend to cancel each other out, and some may even be harmful.

The most important practice is meditation—a word that has by now been applied to so many things that it may very well convey nothing at all. Here, we mean something very specific by the term. Meditation is a way of focusing your mind on a spiritual topic so that your higher senses begin to enter your awareness. This form of meditation is sometimes called "discursive" meditation because, especially at first, it can take the form of an interior discourse or conversation. At first, it may seem like ordinary musing, but it is actually something quite different. Although it is simple, and at times may seem boring, it is one of the most important magical skills you can learn.

On beginning magical work, you may find it very difficult to assess the results you are getting—or even whether or not you are getting results at all. This is one reason it can be much more effective to study with someone who has already done similar kinds of work. One of the more common perplexities arises as a result of doing work with the focus of attention. Students often wonder if some phenomenon they experience is real or illusory. The problem, in many cases, is that there's no straightforward answer to such questions.

One type of exercise involves fixing your gaze on an object for some period of time. If you do this, and really succeed in holding your gaze steady, the object, and indeed much of your visual field, undergoes a kind of transformation, a blanking out—unless, of course, you become startled by the effect and shift your gaze even slightly.

This is a well-known physiological effect of fixing your gaze. Your retina and the nerves that serve it are constructed so that any constant stimulus—that is, any stimulus that occurs precisely and unvaryingly in a particular place on the retina—becomes invisible. This is why you usually do not see the blood vessels that supply the retina, for example. Usually, your eyes are constantly making slight motions, so that even objects that are not moving do not cast their images onto exactly the same place from moment to moment. With relaxation, however, and the fixation of vision that can come with the stabilization of attention, it is not hard to stop this vibrating motion and experience a temporary blanking of vision.

The same thing is true of other sensory systems. A constant touch or constant scent will also disappear—and not simply as a result of "getting used to it," as when background music disappears. Even more important, this is also true of consciousness itself. This point is not as easy to demonstrate, since you are so used to seeing through consciousness that it can be very difficult to bring it into the forefront of your attention. Nevertheless, when the famous English Hermetic magician Dion Fortune described magic as the art of creating "willed changes in consciousness," she was referring not only to changing the contents or quality of consciousness, but also to the possibility of changing what we may call the focal length or tuning of consciousness.

Many types of magical activity effect such changes almost by accident. People can do magic without being able to explain what is happening when things work well or otherwise, like the famous fellow who one day found out that all his life he'd been speaking prose. Since our aim is not simply to teach a bag of tricks, but to preserve and pass on what is a very full magical, meditative, and philosophical tradition, we think it is important to point these things out, even though they may at first seem like very abstract propositions. When these effects of focused attention are seen from the physiological standpoint, they are mere curiosities of the bodily mechanism; understood from the esoteric point of view, however, they can be keys that open doors into an illimitable region of experience and meaning.

This course was written by people who each pursued the study of the Hermetic and magical traditions in a variety of ways. Each of us came to the conclusion that these traditions deserved to be kept alive and not simply be given over, on one hand, to the quibbling of academic critics and, on the other, to the fiddling of magical mechanics and tinkers. None of us claims to be a guru or master—and fortunately, the tradition does not depend on gurus or masters for its continuing life, though its history is studded with great souls whose achievements are undeniable. We see ourselves as students of the Hermetic and magical traditions, hoping to assist other students to appreciate and work with those traditions as fully as possible.

HEBREW AS A MAGICAL LANGUAGE

In most forms of Hermetic high magic, a collection of words and names in Hebrew are used in ritual. You have already experienced one example of this in the Qabalistic Cross, the ritual exercise presented in lesson 2 (see page 38). Another set of Hebrew words and names plays a part in the Lesser Banishing Ritual of the Pentagram, which will be presented in this lesson. While Hebrew may seem an odd choice, the reasons for its use are deeply rooted in history. The most important tradition of ritual magic that became part of the

Hermetic magical synthesis during the Renaissance was Jewish in origin, and the Qabalah, a tradition of Jewish mystical philosophy with deep connections to magic, also entered Hermetic circles during this time. Both these traditions make use of the symbolism of the Hebrew alphabet and certain Hebrew words.

Some wag once observed that a "tradition" in the modern Western esoteric world is any group of people who can agree on how to spell "Qabalah," and this remark has a certain truth to it. If you have studied any Western European language, you know that, even within the group of languages using the "same" alphabet, letters can have very different sounds. This is even truer when going from one alphabet to another, and English presents special difficulties because many of its letters can have several sounds, depending on context.

When Hebrew words were brought into Latin texts during the Renaissance, the usual strategy was to represent the sound of the words as best possible in Roman letters using their Latin values. The spelling "Cabala" dates from this period. The spelling "Kabbalah" is generally used in the academic world, except when referring to the Christianized (or at least de-Judaized) versions of the tradition that developed during the Renaissance; these are often called "Christian Cabala," using the spelling that was used within their texts. The spelling "Qabalah" was developed by 19th-century occultists as a result of a desire to have romanized spellings that reflected the actual Hebrew letters that had originally composed the word. The main impetus here was the need to work with the number-and-letter manipulations of the "literal Qabalah"—a set of methods we'll discuss later in the course.

One of the main conventions is to transliterate the Hebrew letters into Roman letters on a one-to-one, and somewhat arbitrary, basis. This provides some information about what the original letters were, though it doesn't necessarily tell much about how to pronounce the words. We will introduce the Hebrew alphabet and some systematic notes on pronouncing Hebrew words later; at this point, however, we will bring up certain divine and angelic names, most of which should not be difficult to pronounce adequately. We will provide both the conventional transliterations, so that students who have not seen them before can become familiar with them; we'll also supply some notes on pronunciation.

We have chosen to spell the word "Qabalah." We are not writing either as historians or as claimants to authority in the world of Judaica, but as Hermetic magicians. While no spelling is "better" than any other, we have used this one as a way of marking our relationship to the living current of Hermetic and occult Qabalistic teaching.

READING

For this lesson, continue working your way through your assigned reading as described in lesson 2, selecting seven sentences from each chapter and focusing your attention on them one at a time. Work with the third and fourth chapters of your book. As you continue with this practice, try to make it as habitual as possible, so that your chosen sentence surfaces in your awareness by itself when your mind has nothing else to occupy it.

TAROT: THE SMALL CARDS

Set aside half an hour to forty-five minutes for this exercise. Do the exercise a total of four times over the next two weeks; as long as you don't do it more than once a day, you can choose how you space these sessions.

1. Set aside the Major Arcana cards you worked with in Lesson 2, and concentrate on the rest of the deck, the Minor Arcana.
2. Sort out the cards by suit, so that you have all the Swords in one pile, all the Wands in another, and so forth.
3. Lay out the cards as in figure 8 (below), leaving enough space in the center for you to stand. Make sure the cards are properly oriented to the four directions.
4. Step into the circle, and turn to face east.
5. Perform the opening gesture, and do a minute or two of rhythmic breathing (see pages 15 and 37).
6. Focus your attention on the suit of Swords. While focusing on these fourteen cards, summon up all the feelings and thoughts

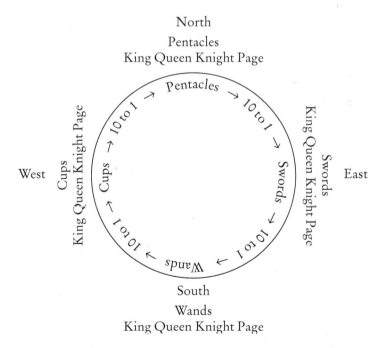

Figure 8. Layout of the small tarot cards.

associated with the east and springtime: the yellow light of sunrise, a freshening breeze, sprouting seedlings, a feeling of clarity and lightness. Let these rise up within you and around you like a sea of energies, and let yourself be immersed in that sea.

7. Keep your attention on the Swords, and remain in the presence of these energies for several minutes; then release the energies, close your eyes, and clear your mind.

8. Turn to face south. Repeat the above process with the suit of Wands and the energies of the south and summer: the heat of noonday, the redness of flame, plants in lush, full growth, a feeling of drive and ambition. After several minutes, release the energies, close your eyes, and clear your mind.

9. Turn to face west, and repeat with the suit of Cups and the energies of autumn: dusk falling, gentle rain, leaves turning color and drifting down from the trees, harvest, fields set to lie fallow for the coming winter. After several minutes, close your eyes, release the energies, and clear your mind.

10. Turn to face north, and repeat with the suit of Pentacles and the energies of winter: a black midnight full of sharp, glittering stars, snow and bare earth, the dark shapes of tree trunks, the storing up and maintenance of what has been harvested. After several minutes, release the energies, close you eyes, and clear your mind.

11. Turn to face east again. Release your awareness from the cards.

12. Close your eyes, clear your mind, and do several minutes of regulated breathing.

13. Perform the closing gesture, collect the cards, and write up your experience in your magical journal.

Meditation

You've now had a month to explore, through the attention practices, the most basic form of the method of meditation you'll use as you work through the course. Depending on your prior experience, and on various subtle factors, you have been more or less successful at clearing and stabilizing your mind, and keeping it focused on the practice. Whatever the results, the experience will be of value in your later work. At this point, however, we present a more complete form. Perform this new practice at least twice a week. Eventually you will meditate every day, but for now, integrate this practice into your week along with the attention practice covered on page 51.

Perform your meditation practice along with a brief version of the relaxation and attention work described on pages 16 and 18, so that it is nested within the pattern of opening, relaxing and breathing, paying attention, and closing. Decide at the beginning of each week when you will meditate; in effect, write it into your daily schedule. If at all possible, never skip these prescheduled sessions, even though your mind will be quite creative in coming up with excuses for doing so. A vital part of the Hermetic way is learning to discipline your mind, and this is an excellent place to begin.

1. Sit in the meditation position given in lesson 1 (see page 19).
2. Let your body relax without losing the balance or symmetry of the position.
3. For approximately five minutes, do the attention practice given on page 18, along with rhythmic breathing (see page 37).
4. When this period is finished, turn your mind to a topic, as described below. Think about it in a general way for a time, and then choose some particular aspect of the topic, or a train

of thought connected with it, and follow that out as far as it will go, considering all the ideas that your mind associates with it.

5. Keep your attention on the subject, lightly but firmly. Your mind should be open enough to allow new ideas to enter, but focused enough to allow you to exclude thoughts that don't have anything to do with the subject.

For example, if the topic for your meditation is the element of earth, you can consider earth as soil, as the source of plant life and growth. This may lead you to think of the yearly cycle of vegetative life, or of fertility in general, and either or both of these may lead to the thought of the lunar cycle, and of the Moon. These ideas in turn may lead you on to others. However far afield the connections go, try to link them back to the original topic and to other ideas you have considered in the course of the meditation.

For this lesson, the topic for your meditations is the four elements: earth, water, fire, and air. Even if you have learned the traditional symbolism of these elements previously, try to focus on the actual physical experience of the elements themselves and let ideas arise from this, rather than from correspondences you may have learned. In this way, you will develop your own personal grasp of the meaning of these important symbols.

For the time being, plan on spending about ten minutes doing actual discursive meditation in each session. When you are finished, repeat a few more cycles of rhythmic breathing and attention, then perform the closing gesture. After each session, note down the ideas that have arisen in connection with the topic, as well as any factors that seemed to help or hinder the meditative process.

Attention

Do the attention exercise for this lesson on each day on which you do not meditate. For approximately the same period, at about the same time, perform the relaxation and attention work of lesson 2 (see page 37). After about five minutes of regulated breathing, however, you may allow your breathing to proceed naturally, without trying to make it stay within any particular pattern. Notice how your attention changes with inhalation and exhalation, and notice when your attention seems to become more focused and when it seems to disperse. When you have achieved some sense of this, recall that energy follows consciousness and feel the alternate ebb and flow of energy through you as you breathe.

As before, use the opening and closing gestures and the initial relaxation to provide a frame for this practice, and write up the results in your practice journal.

Ritual: The Lesser Banishing Ritual of the Pentagram

This ritual exercise, which builds on that of the last lesson, should be done once a day, ideally after the attention exercise or meditation for the day. You may wish to try it after the attention exercise for one week and before the attention exercise for the next week to see whether and how the results vary. This is where the private space with "enough open floor space to allow you to walk in a circle without bumping into furniture" mentioned in lesson 1, is needed.

1. Stand facing east, in the center of the space around which you will trace the pentagrams and perform the Qabalistic Cross (see page 38).

2. Step forward to the east until you reach the circumference of the circle. Extend the first two (middle and index) fingers of your right hand, folding the others into your palm and placing your thumb over them. With these two fingers held together, trace a banishing pentagram in the air (see figure 9 below). Begin at the lower left and draw a line upward to the top, continuing down to the lower right, then to the left arm, the right arm, and back down to the lower left to complete the figure, which should be about three feet across. While tracing, visualize a line of blue-white light being traced by your fingers as they move through the air. Then point to the center of the pentagram and vibrate the divine name *YHVH* ("Ye-ho-wah").

3. From the center of the eastern pentagram, trace a blue-white line a quarter circle around the space until you reach the south. At the southern point of the circle, trace a second banishing pentagram. Then point to the center of the pentagram and vibrate the divine name *ADNI* ("Ah-doh-nai").

4. From the center of the southern pentagram, trace the next

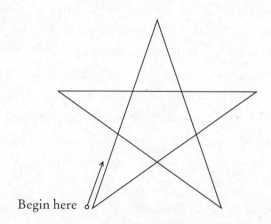

Begin here

Figure 9. Tracing the banishing pentagram.

quarter of the circumference to the western point of the circle; there trace another banishing pentagram, point to its center, and vibrate the Name *AHIH* ("Eh-heh-yeh").

5. From there, tracing the circle as before, continue to the north, trace a banishing pentagram, and, at its center, vibrate the name *AGLA* ("Ah-geh-la").

6. Complete the circle by tracing the line back to the center of the pentagram at the east. Return to the center and face east.

7. Extend your arms horizontally out to the side (toward the north and south), and say:

Before me, Raphael ("Rah-fa-el")
Behind me, Gabriel ("Gah-bree-el")
At my right hand, Michael ("Mee-khah-el")
At my left hand, Auriel ("Oh-ree-el")
For about me flame the pentagrams
And within me shines the six-rayed star.

8. While saying this, visualize the archangels as towering winged figures at the quarters of the circle, radiant with light. Raphael, wearing yellow and purple, carries a sword; Gabriel, wearing blue and orange, carries a cup; Michael, wearing red and green, carries a staff; Auriel, wearing citrine, olive, russet, and black, carries a pentacle (a disk inscribed with a five-pointed star). As you pronounce each name, the figure expands or springs into being from the point at the center of the name at the center of the pentagram, rising a little outward, but with the pentagram somewhat within it. When you refer to the pentagrams, direct your attention to their vivid presence around you. When you speak of the six-rayed star, see a Star of David on your chest,

the upward-pointing triangle in red, the downward-pointing
one in blue.

9. Complete the rite by performing the Qabalistic Cross
   (see page 38).

The Lesser Banishing Ritual of the Pentagram is one of the fundamental rituals of Hermetic high magic, and it should be practiced relentlessly. Its effect, as you will find after a few performances, is to "clear the air" magically, providing a cleansed and protected space in which to perform other magical workings. In full-scale magical ceremonies, it has a crucial role, and other rituals using very similar patterns also come into use quite often in ceremonial working.

LESSON REVIEW

1. Perform the relaxation and attention exercises daily, either with or without a meditation (see pages 16 and 51).
2. Perform the daily recollection each day on going to bed (see page 20).
3. Continue the reading exercise introduced in the last lesson (see page 31).
4. Do the meditation at least once for each of the four elements (see page 49).
5. Do the tarot exercise at least four times (see page 46).
6. Perform the Pentagram Ritual daily, as described on pages 51–54.
7. Keep a record of your work.

When you have spent at least two weeks on this lesson and completed the work listed above, take an extra week to go back over the material covered in the first three lessons. Read them over, along with your entries in your magical journal. If you are not satisfied with the way one of the exercises went, do it over again. In the meantime, continue with the practices from lesson 3, and use the fifth chapter of your book as the material for the reading exercise.

When you finish this weeklong review, you are ready to go on to lesson 4.

LESSON 4

THE SCALE
OF UNITY

With this lesson, the focus of your studies will undergo a certain
amount of change. The emphasis of the last three lessons has been
on the elementary techniques of Western esoteric training. In this
lesson and the lessons to come, however, this emphasis alternates
with a focus on the elementary theory of the tradition. Both of these,
theory and practice, are useful and necessary parts of the work, and
you will find that each reinforces the other. Knowledge of the essential theoretical structure of magic gives context and meaning to the
practical work, while the exercises help turn the theory from a set of
dry intellectual statements to an expression of living realities.

NUMBER SYMBOLISM

One barrier to understanding that modern students of ancient magical traditions must overcome lies in a major shift between ancient
and modern times in ideas about number—what numbers are and
what they mean. To the modern mind, a number is simply a quantity.
It has no particular meaning or importance of its own, and nothing

but quantity sets it apart from any other number. Thus the concept that numbers have a symbolism of their own, a symbolism that is centrally important to magic, seems bizarre to the modern mind.

In ancient thought and magical traditions such as Hermeticism that derive from the ancient world, number is understood in a radically different sense. To this way of thought, any given number is a quality as well as a quantity, with characteristics, imagery, and meanings of its own, wholly apart from anything to which it might be attached as pure quantity. Thus the number three, for example, possesses a quality or flavor of its own, which we may call "threeness." Any time the quantity three appears, the flavor of threeness is present. Anything that naturally occurs in threes or divides into three parts partakes of that same quality. Time — which divides into past, present, and future — and the process of reproduction — which involves mother, father, and child — are thus both linked symbolically and magically with the number three, sharing its quality or flavor, its essential character, and its subtle relationships with other numbers.

Old books of magic contain tables of the "scales" of number symbolism. The term "scale," from Latin *scala*, literally meant "ladder" and suggested the use of such tables as a way to climb to higher modes of consciousness. These tables classified an enormous range of things, natural and supernatural, in terms of the number qualities they expressed. They gained much of their effectiveness, however, from religious and cultural symbolisms that have long since dropped out of use, and the present age has yet to create any coherent set of transformative symbols of its own. Each student of these traditions, therefore, must, to some extent, re-create a symbolic system of this sort using the core principles of magical philosophy to combine the useful elements of traditional systems with other material derived from personal experience. The number exercise in this lesson, and other exercises in lessons to come, help you make a start on this phase of your magical training.

THE NUMBER ONE

The number one may seem straightforward enough, but "one" in this connection is much more than the name for an amount, or the first place in a series. It refers to the quality of unity and all that is implied by it.

A unity is an entity, a thing that is held together in two ways: because all of it shares in being part of the whole, and because it is distinct from everything else. In other words, it is defined, or bounded. It is what it is, and not anything else. This line of thought, by the way, can be traced back through the great systematizing Neoplatonist Proclus, all the way through Plato, to the followers of Pythagoras, the first major historical figure in Western magical traditions. To the casual reader, it can easily seem to be a kind of abstract logic-chopping. In fact, it is something very different. It is one part of an attempt to make systematic sense out of the experiences that arise from meditative and magical explorations.

One way to understand this is to reflect on the part of the soul that corresponds to the number one. The Hebrew word *yechidah*, which is often translated "will," is also related to words that mean "one" and "unity." This suggests the one-pointedness of the will that is so often stressed in magic; but it also, and in some ways more importantly, refers to the unifying act of the will through which we define a situation and our position within it. It is through a clear understanding of this unifying aspect of the will, in fact, that we can grasp what it means for the will to be one-pointed.

If you have a chessboard and a pile of checkers as well as a set of chess pieces, you have the option of playing any number of games. Once you decide to play chess, however, the board loses its indeterminate, open-ended quality; it becomes a chessboard. Once you decide to play chess, all the other kinds of pieces become irrelevant, except to the extent that they can represent (if necessary) chess pieces. It is your intention, or will, to play chess that makes the situation what it is: a chess game, with its own unity, in which all the pieces and the board and even the players participate. As you become absorbed in the game, you do not have to practice special exercises to become one-pointed: you simply follow your intentions and let everything else fall away.

By an act or gesture of will (simple enough, though it presupposes a complex structure of already-established ideas and intentions about chess, the board, the pieces, and the moves) you have brought that game into being. This is what is at the root (or summit) of the Qabalistic Tree of Life: the acts of will, or intention, that from moment to moment and lifetime to lifetime bring into being the fields of action within which you act.

But there is more to the will than that. *Yechidah* refers not only to the will through which you act, but to the will that enacts you. In meditative and magical work, it becomes gradually clearer that, at the root of your being is not only your own will, but your being willed. In the same way that you can constitute a chess game by intending to play it, so you are constituted as an individual with will by another will, which is not your own, but which generates your will by making you a unity.

This constituting will is, in old-fashioned technical terms, the "scintilla" or unfallen spark that links us to the divine. This is mirrored in the divine name of Kether, the first sephirah of the Tree of Life, which means "I will be," and is a shorter form of "I will be that which I will be"—no doubt one of the earliest recorded formulas of existentialism.

KE†HER

Most books on the Qabalah, including those that are part of this course's book list, include a page of various symbols and correspondences associated with each of the ten sephiroth of the Tree of Life. Such correspondences, often drawn up into complicated tables, have been a fixture of Western esoteric writings for hundreds of years. A number of modern magical writers have rejected this sort of thing as useless, but this rejection derives from a misunderstanding of the purpose and nature of correspondences.

The point of these tables is not to load down your mind with materials suitable for some bizarre sort of esoteric Trivial Pursuit. Rather, correspondences serve as a way to unify and organize magical symbolism, to convert the weird grab bag of traditional images and ideas into a coherent alphabet of symbols that can be used to communicate clearly with the deep levels of the mind and the subtle aspects of the universe.

To some extent, the point raised earlier in this lesson in the discussion of number symbolism applies here as well: much of the traditional imagery derived its force from cultural beliefs and habits of thought that have long since fallen into disuse. It thus has limited relevance to the modern student. Certain elements of symbolism are still useful, however, either because they tie into still-living ways of thought, because they link up to basic aspects of human existence, or because the surviving materials of the magical tradition are all but incomprehensible without them. These symbols include the sephirah's traditional name and divine name, its associated archangel and order of angels, and its astrology and tarot correspondences. It is with this rather more limited set of symbols that you will work at this stage in your magical training. The role of each of them in magical practice will become clearer as we proceed.

SYMBOLISM OF KETHER

For this lesson's work, your assignment is to learn a selection of symbols associated with Kether, the Crown, the first sephirah. These are as follows:

Divine name: *AHIH* (pronounced "Eh-heh-yeh"), "I Am"

Archangel: Metatron, Prince of the Countenances

Angelic order: Chaioth ha-Qodesh, "Holy Living Creatures"

Astrological correspondence: Rashith ha-Gilgalim, "Beginnings of Turnings" or *Primum Mobile*, identified with the galaxy as the background of stellar and planetary forces

Tarot correspondence: the four aces of the deck

You must not only familiarize yourself with these correspondences, but commit them to memory; as you proceed with your magical training, they will become more and more important.

Finally, write four of these symbols onto the large Tree of Life you made back in lesson 2 (see page 35). In the innermost of the four circles of Kether, write in the divine name and its meaning; in the next, the archangel; in the next, the angelic order; and in the outermost circle, the astrological correspondence. The end result will look something like figure 10 (see page 63).

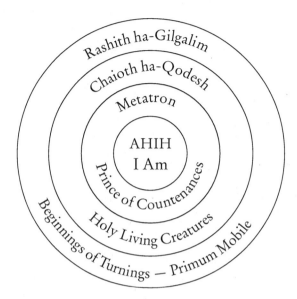

Figure 10. The symbols of Kether inscribed on the circles.

Once you have written in the symbols, use a white colored pencil to color in the rest of the space, or simply leave the space blank.

THE ELEVENTH, TWELFTH, AND THIRTEENTH PATHS

Along with the symbolism of Kether itself, you must commit to memory the symbolism and meanings of the three paths on the Tree of Life that extend down from Kether to lower sephiroth of the Tree. These are the eleventh, twelfth, and thirteenth paths, which are assigned to the first three letters of the Hebrew alphabet and the first three Major Arcana of the tarot deck.

The relationship of the paths to the sephiroth is complex, and subject to a range of common misunderstandings. For the time being, you can simply think of the paths as the routes or transitions that allow passage from one sephirah to another. This passage can be made in two directions—from above, as energy descends to create the cosmos, and from below, as created beings rise up along the paths of spiritual and magical attainment.

The symbolism of the first three paths is as follows:

Eleventh path

Location on the Tree: Kether to Chokmah

Hebrew letter: א, Aleph

Tarot correspondence: Trump 0, the Fool

Astrological correspondence: the element of air

Twelfth path

Location on the Tree: Kether to Binah

Hebrew letter: ב, Beth

Tarot correspondence: Trump I, the Magician

Astrological correspondence: Mercury

Thirteenth path

Location on the Tree: Kether to Tiphareth

Hebrew letter: ג, Gimel

Tarot correspondence: Trump II, the High Priestess

Astrological correspondence: Moon

All these symbols have further implications of their own, but these can be left until later, or studied in textbooks of Qabalistic theory.

For now, simply concentrate on learning the symbols. Just as it is impossible to read effectively until you have learned to recognize the letters of the alphabet without thinking about them—an act of learning that requires the use of memory—it is impossible to progress far in magic without learning the symbolic alphabet of the art. Work put into this task now will pay substantial dividends later on.

READING

You have now been practicing the special approach to reading given in lesson 2 for about five weeks, and it's time to take a moment to look back at what you've done and why. During this time, you have interacted with five chapters from a magical text in several different ways. Ordinary reading is the first of these. Second is a much more careful, analytical mode of reading, set in motion by asking yourself to sort through the sentences of each chapter and select seven that communicate the essential points of the chapter. Third is the process of mulling over the sentences you've selected, thinking about their meanings. Fourth is a deeper, less visible form of consideration that goes on in the deep places of your mind when you are focused on a concept by some of the tactics we have taught in earlier lessons.

All of this work aims at three results. First, it forces you to engage the text you are reading far more intensively than you usually do, and to think about the ideas contained in each chapter. Second, it makes you a good deal more familiar with some of the basic ideas of Hermetic magic than you were before you started. Both of these are extremely useful in your magical training.

The third result is a little wider in scope. Most people, most of the time, let their surroundings fill their minds with chatter from the moment they wake up to the moment they fall asleep. Entire industries exist to help us keep our heads packed with irrelevancies, while life slips past us and a world full of magic and wonder goes by unnoticed.

The third point of the reading exercise is to make a very modest beginning at another way of life. By turning your mind, gently but repeatedly, toward ideas that mean something and insights that can reshape your way of looking at the world, you take a first step toward shaping an inner life that is not simply a collection of unthinking responses to the world around you.

This process of reshaping can be a source of some conflict, not only because of the ingrained habits of the human mind, but also because the chatter that fills most minds has the function of distracting attention from unresolved problems and issues. Still, mental clarity and self-knowledge are both essentials of the magical path, and this exercise (along with others that will be introduced later) is a relatively gentle way to begin moving toward these goals.

In this lesson's work, your first reading exercise is to read back over the five chapters you've explored in this way, then go on to read the sixth chapter of your book. Pay attention to the experience of reading; note any differences in the way your mind handles the flow of ideas from the book. Notice also if there's a difference between reading chapters you've worked through and reading one that you haven't.

Your second reading exercise is to proceed as before, selecting seven sentences from each chapter as you come to it, and keeping company with one of those sentences on each day of the following week. You will continue this process throughout the nine months you spend on this course. When you finish one book, go on to one of the others. As always, make notes on your experiences in your magical journal.

NUMBER EXERCISE

It's important to start to work directly with the numerical approach to symbolism described earlier. The number you'll work with in this lesson, of course, is the number one. Your task is to notice and think about everything in your experience that can be described by, or that is linked with, this number. You may find it useful to keep a list, either in your magical journal or elsewhere, of all the manifestations of the number one in your life.

You can pursue this exercise in one very productive direction by noticing those things that don't seem to have unities involved with them, and finding the hidden unity at work. It's common, for instance, to think of two sides of a quarrel or two opposing viewpoints in a controversy as complete opposites, with nothing connecting them at all. Nearly always this is an illusion, and the two sides have far more in common than either one is willing to admit. Make it a habit, whenever you are confronted with some sort of extreme opposition, to look for the unrecognized unities. The result can be illuminat-ing—and often useful in the most practical terms. As always, keep notes on the results of your work in your magical journal.

MEDITATION

The method of meditation introduced in lesson 3 can be expanded and elaborated in many ways. For the time being, however, it will be of more value in your training to develop a certain level of skill with the basic technique and with its use as a means of working with the traditional symbolism.

For this lesson, therefore, your meditation follows the same format and process presented in lesson 3 (see page 49). Only the topic will be different. Rather than working with the four elements in general, explore a specific aspect of their energies through the medium of the tarot.

- When you have finished the preliminaries to meditation and are ready to begin working with the topic, call to mind one of the four aces of the deck. Picture it in your mind's eye as clearly as possible, putting as many of the card's details into the image as you can.
- Consider the image and think about its possible meanings. This image represents the way that the number one, the principle of unity, manifests through one of the elements. What does it communicate to you?
- Be ready to draw on your previous meditations on the elements, as well as the tarot exercise on page 46 and this lesson's readings to build up your sense of the symbol's meaning.
- Be ready, too, to go out on a limb if your intuition leads you there. The conclusions you reach at this point in your training are less important than the experience of reaching them. Symbols such as these mean something a little different to everyone who works with them.

One of the goals of these meditations is to come to a clearer understanding of the meanings of the tarot aces. When you finish meditating on each of the aces, therefore, look for a single word that, for you, sums up the card and its qualities as you understand them. For example, "power" may be the word that best describes the Ace of Wands to you, or "unity," while "matter" or "manifestation" may best fit the Ace of Pentacles. Commit the words you select to memory.

Do at least four of these meditations during the next two weeks so that all four of the aces and elements are covered; you can do the meditations more frequently if you wish, up to once a day. Begin with the Ace of Pentacles for earth, then the Ace of Swords for air, then the Ace of Cups for water, and finish with the Ace of Wands for fire. As with the last lesson's meditation, ten minutes of actual discursive meditation should be sufficient for each practice session.

Repeat the attention exercise given in lesson 3 on any day in which you do not do a meditation as described above. Review the instructions in lesson 2 (see page 37) to make sure you have not forgotten details of the practice.

RITUAL

Perform the Lesser Banishing Ritual of the Pentagram given in lesson 3 each day. As you work with this rite over the next two weeks, concentrate on making the visualized images as clear and bright as you can. Here, too, you may find it useful to review the instructions given in lesson 3 and adjust your performance as necessary.

LESSON REVIEW

1. Perform the meditation or the attention exercise each day (see pages 67 and 51).
2. Perform the daily recollection each day on going to bed (see page 20).
3. Perform the Lesser Banishing Ritual of the Pentagram each day (see page 51).
4. Perform the reading exercise each day (see page 31).

5. Work on the number exercise described above throughout the next two weeks.

6. Keep a record of your work.

When you have worked on this lesson for at least two weeks and have completed the work listed above, you are ready to proceed to lesson 5.

LESSON 5

THE POWER
OF DUALITY

Concepts of power or energy have a central place in ideas about magic commonly found among those uneducated in it. From "The Force" and its equivalents in fantasy and science fiction, through notions of magical or occult "powers" current in our culture, to the continuing if largely fruitless efforts of parapsychologists to find detectable energies at work in psychic phenomena, these concepts pervade modern thinking on the subject. This is understandable, since technologies developed out of a scientific worldview provide modern minds with their principal metaphors for magic.

Magic, however, is not a technology. It does not base itself on, or justify itself through, scientific models of the universe. The secret of attaining "magical powers" is not a matter of finding some sort of socket of cosmic energy and inserting the right kind of plug. In fact, the idea that magic has primarily to do with gaining power or powers is largely a modern construction, having little or nothing to do either with authentic traditions of magic on the one hand, or the experience of magical practice on the other.

It is important to grasp this point and grasp it well, because some of the material covered in this lesson and the next can too easily be misinterpreted in terms of these common cultural habits of thought. Concepts of energy do have a place in the traditional lore of magic, although the concepts differ significantly from those of science. This lesson presents some of these concepts. In subsequent lessons, we'll explore several ways of working with energy in the magical sense. In dealing with all this material, pay attention to the assumptions you may be carrying, and to the possibility of misunderstandings based on them. This will keep you from some common mistakes.

LEVELS OF BECOMING

One way to understand the magical concept of energy lies in the system of five levels of being presented in lesson 2. This scheme mapped out five phases of existence, with pure spirit or potentiality at one end, and pure matter or manifestation at the other. If you are not sure you understand the system clearly at this point, review pages 25 through 31 before reading further.

This system appears static, like a layer cake of five layers. At a deeper level of understanding, however, it is anything but that. Each of the five phases interacts with the others, directly and indirectly; each emerges out of others and in turn produces others. This complex web of processes can be symbolized, in a somewhat simplified form, as a system of energy flows.

In this system, the primary flow—like the main current of a river, in which other eddies and currents are carried along—is from the spiritual to the material. Patterns emerge out of the pure potentiality of spirit, take on progressively more concrete shapes as they descend through the levels, and finally come into complete manifestation in the realm of matter. This flow is the driving force of the creation of the universe, which, in magical teachings, is a continuous process rather than a once-and-for-all event at the beginning of time.

The descending flow of creative energy is also, in a sense, the primary secret of magic. Everything at the material level of being represents the endpoint of a pattern moving down the planes, and is created and sustained by that pattern. If the pattern can be shaped at another level, therefore, the material manifestation will change accordingly, to the extent that the inertia of the realm of matter will permit. The methods of magic, then, can be seen on one level as ways of taking hold of a descending current of creative force and shaping it in accordance with will.

In addition to this descending flow, however, there is another that balances it, moving in the opposite direction: from matter to spirit, from fixed manifestation toward free potentiality. This ascending flow emerges from the farthest point of matter and returns to its opposite at the farthest point of spirit, forming a cycle. The descending flow drives the process of creation; the ascending flow is responsible for the process of redemption—the return of the individual being to wholeness and freedom. The descending flow is the primary secret of magic; the ascending flow is the primary secret of mysticism. A traditional Qabalistic saying has it that Malkuth causes an impulse to flow from the Prince of Countenances in Kether, which summarizes much of what can be said about magic. A corresponding mystical teaching sees the mystical impulse as triggered by an act of grace from above.

In the lessons to come, you will learn ways to work with these two currents in various ways, not all of them obvious. For now, think about them and what they imply. What parts of your experience of the world may support these ideas? What parts may contradict them?

THE MAGICAL WILL

The concept of the magical will has already been discussed in this course, and will be discussed again. Since the time of Eliphas Levi, whose writings on magic launched the modern revival of the subject, magical circles have widely recognized that the training of the will is essential to any form of inner development. This has given rise, however, to a series of misunderstandings. Victorian ideas of "willpower" as jaw-clenching, white-knuckled inner conflict have become widely confused with the very different nature of will as magical philosophy understands it.

It should be obvious at once that the inner struggle of the Victorian model is a sign of the comparative weakness of will, not of its strength. Gritted teeth and clenched fists, in addition to being a waste of muscular effort, show that the will has met resistance of a strength comparable to its own. When the will is sufficiently strong, it accomplishes its goals effortlessly and without strain.

It is important to distinguish between several different characteristics of the will. Sheer strength of will—the ability to hold to an intention despite distractions and resistance—is one of these, but it is by no means the only one of importance. Skillful direction of will is another. In most things in life, a very modest amount of effort intelligently applied reaps greater rewards than a vast outpouring of effort poorly aimed. A strong man may be able to kick his way through a door, but it's a good deal less wasteful of energy (and of doors) to simply turn the knob and push.

Moreover, will directed in harmony with the natural flow of things is generally much more effective than will turned against that flow. This is an important element of magical ethics, and a subject that will occupy some space in future lessons.

THE NUMBER TWO: CHOKMAH

In the same way that one refers to unity and to unification (to making things one and to being made one thing), two refers to duality and division. In cosmological or mythological terms, this is described in terms of the emergence of two, or duality, out of one, or unity. This emergence is often described in terms of an unself-conscious awareness becoming aware of itself, and thus becoming double; the awareness becomes conscious of its own image, while the image equally comes to include the fact of self-awareness. Thus, in a sense, each becomes aware of the other.

This rather abstract notion has some very concrete parallels. In a relationship between two people, for example, in which others are in one way or another shut out or irrelevant, there are not only two people, but two kinds of experience. If I am speaking with one other person, for example, I can be aware of the other person, or I can be aware of the other person's being aware of me. I become aware that there are, in fact, two versions of me. One is the object of my own awareness; the other is the object of the other person's awareness. There is awareness from the inside and awareness from the outside, and both of us have both kinds. Furthermore, it is impossible to have an encounter between two people in which this does not occur, although it is certainly possible for people to lose track of that fact.

This emergence of doubleness out of a unified situation is what the technical language of magic calls "polarity." The word is often used rather loosely to describe any situation in which there are two components, and it is also used very narrowly to refer to the particular sort of polarized situation in which sexuality, in some sense, is involved. Its essential meaning, however, goes somewhat deeper, referring to the development of duality out of a prior unity. For example, any loaf of bread that you see has a left and a right side. But no matter how you slice it, you can't get a slice of bread that has only a left side and no right side. Once a unity is made manifest, duality arises—if only out of the act of definition that draws the boundary that makes the thing what it is.

This is mirrored in the divine name associated with Chokmah, the second sephirah on the Tree of Life. This is *YH* or *Yah*, composed of two Hebrew letters, Y (yod, associated with fire, and primordially active) and H (heh, associated with water, and primordially passive or receptive). The name embodies the polarization of consciousness into subject and object, a polarization that springs into being as soon as consciousness is differentiated.

SYMBOLISM OF CHOKMAH

In this lesson, as in the last, you will learn a selection of the symbols attributed to the second sephirah, Chokmah, Wisdom. These are as follows:

Divine name: YH (pronounced "Yah")

Archangel: Ratziel, "Secret of God"

Angelic order: Auphanim, "Wheels"

Astrological correspondence: Mazloth, the Zodiac

Tarot correspondence: the four twos of the deck

As before, commit these correspondences to memory. (You can do this by making flash cards with the name of the sephirah on one side and the correspondences on the other.) Write the divine name, archangel, angelic order, and astrological correspondence on the four circles of Chokmah on your Tree of Life diagram, then color the sephirah gray.

THE FOURTEENTH, FIFTEENTH, AND SIXTEENTH PATHS

As discussed in lesson 4, you must also learn the basic symbolism of the paths in the process of working through this course. The paths assigned to this lesson are the three that descend from Chokmah to other sephiroth of the Tree. These paths and their symbols are as follows:

Fourteenth path

Location on the Tree: Chokmah to Binah

Hebrew letter: ד, Daleth

Tarot correspondence: Trump III, the Empress

Astrological correspondence: Venus

Fifteenth path

Location on the Tree: Chokmah to Tiphareth

Hebrew letter: ה, Heh

Tarot correspondence: Trump IV, the Emperor

Astrological correspondence: Aries

Sixteenth path

Location on the Tree: Chokmah to Chesed

Hebrew letter: ו, Vau

Tarot correspondence: Trump V, the Hierophant

Astrological correspondence: Taurus

One useful way to learn these, and to associate them with other aspects of magical symbolism, is to use the corresponding tarot trumps as flash cards to test your memory. Sort out the trumps that correspond to paths you have learned, draw one at random, and practice repeating the path, Hebrew letter, and astrological factor corresponding to that card at once, without having to think about it. With time and practice, your mind will connect the imagery of the tarot card automatically with the other correspondences associated with it— a process that will assist substantially in certain important areas of magical work.

READING

Your reading exercise for the two weeks you spend on this lesson follows the same lines as in previous lessons. As before, read one chapter from your book each week and locate seven important sentences from the chapter, each of which will be your focus for one day of that week. During the time you spend on this lesson, make a particular effort to keep the sentence for each day in the background of your mind as you go about your daily round.

NUMBER EXERCISE

The material and exercise on number symbolism covered in lesson 4 gave you a first glance at this aspect of the traditional lore—and, perhaps, a more personal sense of the meanings of unity. This lesson's work is intended to expand on both of these.

For the next two weeks, you'll work with the number two. Your task is to notice and think about everything in your experience that can be described by or linked with this number. As before, you may find it useful to keep a list in your practice journal or elsewhere.

The number two appears in certain noticeably different forms. Some dualities—light and shadow, for example—are formed from the presence and absence of a single thing; others—up and down, for instance— are relative positions along a single scale or continuum; still others—male and female are an example here—are complementary functions of a single process. Other classes may suggest themselves to you as well. As always, keep notes on your work in your practice journal.

WILL EXERCISE

Discussions of the magical will often make this particular faculty of the self sound like some mysterious force to be developed by complicated exercises. In actuality, will itself is far from mysterious, and the exercises used to develop it are extremely simple. Nonetheless, such exercises are important in magical training.

It is important to understand the distinction that texts about magic often make between the higher and lower will. The higher will, which has been discussed at length already, is the essential intentionality or constituting will of the self—the orientation toward the world that, to make use of the metaphor discussed above, leads one person to treat it as a game of chess while another sees it as a game of checkers. The lower will is the (usually) more conscious process of applying intentionality to specific events or objects in the universe of experience. The difference between the two is largely a matter of perception, and has more reality at basic levels of magical training than it does later on. To the adept, the higher and lower wills are not different things. To the novice, however, they are distinct, and this distinction needs to be outgrown, not simply rejected. Meanwhile, the lower will itself can be made the subject of useful forms of magical training.

In an important sense, power of will is simply a habit, and one that can be developed by simple practice. You either get in the habit of making a choice and then following through on it or you don't. Many of the 19th-century manuals of will training (and there was once a whole literature on this subject) recognized this and counseled the student to start off with exercises in which there was no chance of failure.

Once you have established the habit of will, you can attempt more difficult tasks. Leave any situations in which emotions or important issues are involved alone until your habit of will is solidly established, so that other factors don't interfere with your simple exercise of will. For the same reason, deliberately pointless actions have always been considered best for this sort of work. It is especially good at first to avoid exercises that have any moral involvement, simply because such things are often closely involved with feelings of pride and shame, or self-blame and self-congratulation, which get in the way of actually doing the work. The whole process is much the same as the early training of a novice weightlifter, who begins with lighter weights and gradually moves on to heavier ones.

This lesson's exercises include this simple practice, which was once a standard introductory exercise in the training of the will. Stand on one side of a room, choose a spot on the wall on the other side, walk across the room, and touch the spot with your hand. Turn around and repeat. Do this a total of ten times per training session, once a day, for the two weeks you spend on this lesson.

MEDITATION

This lesson's meditative work follows the same pattern introduced in lesson 4. The one difference is that, for the next two weeks, the topic of your meditative work is the four twos of the tarot. These can be seen as symbols of the expression of Chokmah, the second sephirah, through the four elements and Four Worlds. As before, work with one card in each meditation session, and feel free to draw on this lesson's readings and your other studies.

You may also find it useful at this point to go back over the instructions on meditation given in lessons 3 and 4, and compare these with what you have been doing. Memory can be a tricky thing, and the mind is capable of twisting even the clearest of material into strange shapes.

As you did with the aces, come up with a single word that expresses the meaning of each of the twos as you understand it and commit these words to memory.

Do at least four sessions of meditation over the two weeks you spend on this lesson, and more than this minimum is useful. As before, every day in which you do not do a meditation, do the relaxation and attention drill given in lesson 3 (see page 51).

RITUAL

Perform the Lesser Banishing Ritual of the Pentagram given on page 51 each day. As you work with this rite over the next two weeks, pay particular attention to changes in the way the space around you feels before, during, and after each portion of the ritual.

LESSON REVIEW

1. Perform the meditation or the attention exercise each day (see pages 81 and 51).
2. Perform the daily recollection each day on going to bed (see page 20).
3. Perform the Lesser Banishing Ritual of the Pentagram each day (see page 51).
4. Perform the reading exercise each day (see page 31).
5. Work on the number exercise described above over the next two weeks.
6. Perform the will exercise described above each day.
7. Keep a record of your work.

When you have worked on this lesson for at least two weeks and have completed the exercises given above, you are ready to proceed to lesson 6.

LESSON 6

MACROCOSM AND MICROCOSM

Every way of thinking about the world—scientific, religious, or magical—defines a relationship between the individual and the universe as a whole. Sometimes these definitions are explicit. More often, they are unstated and link up in unexpected ways with the worldview that underlies them. Medieval notions of the place of humanity in the cosmos followed the rigid hierarchical structure of medieval society, with God as a sort of ultimate feudal monarch and human beings as vassals of varying ranks owing him fealty and service.

In a similar fashion, current scientific notions about matter are reflected in the most common ways of thinking about what it means to be human. The autonomous individual, affecting society through mass actions such as voting or membership in an organization, is an exact mirror of the atom moving on its path through empty space, affecting the world we experience only when it combines with millions of others. (It's worth noting that the roots of the words "individual" and "atom" mean exactly the same thing.)

The Western esoteric tradition similarly defines a specific way of understanding the relationship between the individual and the universe. Where the two systems mentioned above have kept their definitions largely implicit, however, the traditional lore of magic includes its own definition as an explicit and essential principle of its teaching.

In Western esoteric thought, the universe and the individual are seen as reflections of each other, related through an identity of structure. In traditional terms, the macrocosm ("great universe"), the cosmos as a whole, and the microcosm ("little universe"), the individual, are alike in nature.

From the modern perspective, which is used to looking at both the self and the world in largely material terms, this idea can look strange to say the least. In terms of their physical structure, certainly, the cosmos and the individual seem to have little in common. (Does the universe have feet?) Behind the apparent bizarreness of the idea, however, are two perceptions crucial to a magical understanding of the world and the self.

The first is the realization that, as human beings, we approach the universe through the medium of human senses and a human mind, and what we perceive is, to a great extent, determined by the nature and limitations of the body as an instrument of our perceptions. On the most basic level, we do not directly sense radio waves, cosmic rays, or any of a vast array of energies flowing through the world around us. Our senses draw on only a tiny fraction of the total range of available stimuli, and then only in tightly channeled and limited ways. More subtly, our brains tend to follow rigid, inborn patterns of perception and thought to a much greater extent than we often realize, particularly where survival, reproduction, and social dominance—aspects of life we share with the animal realm—are concerned. The universe we perceive, then, is largely shaped by, and even reflected from, who we are.

The second of these perceptions is the realization that certain aspects of the universe, as traditional magical thought understands it, are mirrored in or from corresponding aspects of the human self. To shift metaphors, universe and self resonate together like tuned strings on a musical instrument, which are of different lengths but relate to a common proportion. The most important of these resonances or proportions, for our purposes, is the recognition of different levels of being in the universe.

LEVELS OF SELF

The system of five levels of being presented in lesson 2 and explored further in lesson 5 thus has a precise analog in the inner structure of the human individual. This mirroring of structure is not merely a matter of abstract theory; it can be shown directly, by a simple process of self-observation.

Take a moment to consider this complicated thing you call "me." Turn your attention to yourself. What do you perceive? Most likely, the first thing you notice is your physical body, your skin, flesh, bones. This shape of dense matter is the analog of the physical level of being in the universe.

Next, move your hand or the muscles of your face; observe the act of will expressed through the physical structure. Note your state of health, not in terms of symptoms, but as a general feeling-state. Rub your palms together for a half-minute or so, then hold them, slightly cupped, a foot apart in front of your chest and move them slightly toward and away from each other, paying careful attention to the sensations.

These are all manifestations of one aspect or another of the etheric level of the self, the intermediate level between your physical body and the more concrete levels of your mind. Of all the levels of the self, this one is certainly the least understood or even noticed in our culture. In fact, many prominent scientists can be reduced to spluttering indignation by the mere mention of such so-called "vitalistic" ideas. Nonetheless, the etheric level of the self can be perceived, strengthened, and used as a means of action just as much as the physical level. Many martial arts, in particular, have raised the technique of training the etheric side of the self to a high level of effectiveness.

From these considerations, turn your attention to the part of you that has been reading these words. Think about your phone number. How did the memory appear in your mind? As a visual image, a voice speaking the numbers, or in some other form? Think about a nearby room, a person you know, an emotion you once felt, something you intend to do tomorrow. What form did these perceptions take in your awareness? Thoughts and feelings of this sort, expressed in concrete sensory forms, make up the concrete consciousness, the level of human experience that corresponds to the astral level of being.

Behind these, however, is another class of inner perceptions that do not have a sensory element. Abstract rather than concrete, they inform and underlie the operations of concrete thinking. Like the etheric level, this level of perceptions is often not used or noticed in our present culture, but, like the etheric level, it can be experienced and developed.

For a glimpse of it, consider the words you are reading right now. They relate to each other in specific ways to produce meaning in your mind. Unless you have recently taken a grammar class (or have an unusually good memory), you will probably not be able to describe more than a few of the rules that govern those relationships; nonetheless, some part of you knows them and applies them to every word you read. This is one function of the abstract consciousness, the analog in yourself of the mental level of being.

Finally, turn your attention away from all these perceptions for a moment, and toward that which perceives them. When you read a word, something experiences the meaning; when you hear a sound, something registers the sensation. Formless and intangible, it forms the background to every perception and every state of consciousness. This inner awareness is the reflection of the spiritual level of being in the human individual.

These five levels of the microcosm are sometimes described as "bodies"; in magical writings, talk about the "astral body" or the "etheric body" is a common feature. This can be a useful shorthand, and it also stresses the real similarities between these levels of the self. You must remember, however, that any system of rigidly divided levels is a simplification and, to some extent, a distortion of a much more fluid reality.

No one system is "true," if that word implies that all others are incomplete or false. Rather, each of the many ways of mapping out the mirrored structures of self and universe are convenient for some uses, awkward for others. They are, ultimately, tools—and possession of a hammer does not necessarily make a screwdriver useless.

THE NUMBER THREE: BINAH

As with one and two, three is not merely a quantity, but a quality—one that can be approached by reflecting on the connection of that quality with consciousness and with your own experience. One of the features of duality, when you see it in terms of human relationships, is the endless cascade of doubling that can occur. For example: I am aware of you and you of me; I am aware of me and of your awareness of me;

you are aware of yourself and of my awareness of you. Or, similarly, a loaf of bread has a left side and a right side; when you cut it once, the piece on the left has a left and a right side, and the piece on the right has a left and a right side. There's no end to it, just an expanding proliferation of pairs, every boundary generating two more.

It is with three that structure emerges, and with it, the possibility of stability. With three people, the third person can see the relationship of the other two as a unity, from the outside, without generating the mirroring cascade that the members of the dyad engender as they make images of their interaction and interact with those images. And each person is a third to the other two. Once this configuration appears, as philosophers and psychoanalysts have recognized, the seeds of the eternal human drama of loyalty and betrayal have been planted.

When you are simply conscious of yourself, and conscious of being conscious of yourself, you wobble back and forth between the two possibilities. But when you recognize both possibilities as a set, you have, in a sense, stood outside them—and suddenly your ability to take yourself as an object of consciousness itself becomes an object of consciousness. You have created a triadic configuration, have reunified the doubleness that emerged out of the original unity.

This movement of consciousness is mirrored in the first part of the divine name associated with Binah, the third sephirah of the Qabalistic Tree of Life. It begins with the letters that constitute the name of Chokmah (I, fire, and H, water), but goes on to V (vau, which corresponds to air, a reflection of the original I that also incorporates H). There is, of course, the fourth letter, another H. This, corresponding as it does to the element earth, represents the final crystallization or solidification of the form that has emerged out of the interaction of the three.

It is in this sense that Chokmah, as wisdom, is linked with two: it is participatory, it involves knowing from within. Binah, as understanding, is objective; it is knowing from without. Binah is the root of the possibility of objective awareness — knowing something as an object, without any sense that it is looking back. Binah is thus the root of the possibility of form.

It is a commonplace of some systems of magical philosophy that everything in the universe consists of a unity that divides into a binary of two factors and is resolved and balanced into a ternary by a third. This concept, sometimes called the law of the ternary, has a wide range of applications. In reproduction, a species (the unity) is differentiated into two sexes (the binary) in order to produce offspring (the ternary). In democratic politics, a nation (the unity) divides into liberal and conservative parties (the binary), which hammer out laws and policies by a process of compromise (the ternary).

Remove any of the elements and the entire process collapses. If the basic unity of a nation breaks down, if only a single party is allowed access to power, or if one or both parties are unwilling to compromise, the entire system of democracy falls apart. Here again, the number three fulfills its role as the basis of form and manifestation.

SYMBOLISM OF BINAH

In this lesson, as in the last two, you will learn a selection of the symbols that are traditionally assigned to third sephirah on the Tree of Life. The symbols are as follows:

Divine name: *YHVH ALHIM* (pronounced "Yehowah Elohim")

Archangel: Tzaphqiel, "Contemplation of God"

Angelic order: Aralim, "Valiant Ones"

Astrological correspondence: Shabbatai, the planet Saturn

Tarot correspondence: the four threes of the deck

As before, commit these correspondences to memory. As you do so review the correspondences of Kether and Chokmah as well. Write the first four of these symbols into the four circles of Binah on your Tree of Life diagram, then color the background of the sephirah black.

THE SEVENTEENTH AND EIGHTEENTH PATHS

As with the last two lessons, you must learn the basic symbolism of a selection of paths of the Tree of Life. The specific paths are the two that descend from Binah to lower sephiroth of the Tree:

Seventeenth path

Position on the Tree: Binah to Tiphareth

Hebrew letter: ז, Zayin

Tarot correspondence: Trump VI, the Lovers

Astrological correspondence: Gemini

Eighteenth path

Position on the Tree: Binah to Geburah

Hebrew letter: ח, Cheth

Tarot correspondence: Trump VII, the Chariot;

Astrological correspondence: Cancer

As mentioned earlier, you may find it useful to use the tarot trumps as flash cards to help you commit these correspondences to memory.

READING

Your reading assignment in this lesson follows the same lines as in the last two. Read one chapter in your book each week, select seven sentences from the chapter and make one a focus of your attention for each day during the week.

As you work on this lesson, pay special attention to the time just before you go to sleep. As you read the sentence that will be your focus for the next day, keep your mind as still and as receptive as possible. If you finish your daily recollection before falling asleep, call the sentence back to memory and allow it to remain before your awareness as you drift off to sleep. In the morning, call the sentence back to mind and see if the deeper levels of yourself have gone to work on it while your conscious self was asleep. If you remember any dreams, see if they are related to the sentence in any way.

It's actually possible to learn to use the hours of sleep as a form of meditation, in which symbols and concepts are absorbed and contemplated while your waking mind slumbers. The reading exercise used in this course provides one way to develop this useful skill.

NUMBER EXERCISE

The work with number symbolism in the last two lessons has, we hope, given you a certain basic sense of the ways in which philosophers and magicians of the past thought of the world in terms of number. This lesson's work is intended to build on this sense.

For the next two weeks, focus your work on the number three. As before, notice and think about those things in your experience that can be described by or are in some way linked with this number. As before, keep a list in your practice journal or elsewhere.

The numbers one and two are, to a great extent, so basic to our experience of the world that it is difficult not to see them everywhere. In fact, the ancient Pythagorean philosophers, whose insights into number became the foundation for the entire structure of numerical symbolism in the West, considered one and two to be so abstract and undefined that, in a sense, they could not be considered "numbers" at all. This is considerably less true with three and the numbers following it.

Threes in the world are still relatively easy to find, but they tend to be confined to much more specific areas of experience. Like the sephirah Binah to which it is linked, the number three tends toward a certain limitation in its expressions—and the numbers beyond three partake of the same limitation, just as all the sephiroth below Binah are conditioned by the restrictive power of the third sephirah.

Note also that the number three appears more often than any other in folktales and legends of the Western world and of many other cultures as well. Genies' wishes, fairies with blessings, brothers setting out on a quest, and many other things in such stories come in threes more often than in any other number. In the study of folklore, a repeated numerical structure like this is called a pattern number. While three is by no means the only such pattern number in the folklore of the Western world, and many non-Western cultures use different pattern numbers (for example, four predominates in Native American legends, and five is common in Chinese folklore), three holds a dominant position in the traditions of the world.

WILL EXERCISE

The exercise for developing the magical will introduced in lesson 5 gave you a taste of the type of will training used in Hermetic magic. It represents the dynamic form of will—the decision to accomplish some action, followed by its accomplishment. There is also a static form of will that is also useful to develop—the decision not to do something for a specific period, followed by its accomplishment.

To experiment with this form of will training, sit in your usual posture of meditation in a place where you can see a clock without moving your head or your eyes. Your task is to remain as motionless as possible. Only the minimum movement necessary to keep breathing is allowed.

Many students find this a far more challenging exercise than the previous one. The body and mind alike seem to rebel against it: muscles ache and cramp, itches and discomforts spring up, whatever posture you are in starts to feel grossly distorted, and any number of good reasons to change position or go somewhere else surface in your mind.

There are good reasons for all these discomforts and distractions. The physical body serves as a dumping ground for unresolved tensions and stresses, and constant movement and fidgeting help keep these from breaking through into consciousness. Stillness removes the veil and allows these to be clearly felt. This is uncomfortable, but essential; only when your body is relaxed and at ease can it function as an effective basis for magical action.

In carrying out this exercise, always decide in advance how long you are going to remain motionless, and then stick to it. Aim low rather than high at first; one minute of stillness, carried out successfully and with strong concentration, will accomplish much more than ten minutes of half-hearted attempts to keep yourself from fidgeting too visibly. Do this exercise at least four times over the next two weeks; as always, write up the results in your magical journal.

MEDITATION

This lesson's meditative work continues along the lines set out in lesson 4. For the next two weeks, the topic of your meditations will be the four threes of the tarot. These can be understood as expressions of Binah through the four elements and Four Worlds. As before, work with one card in each session of meditation, and feel free to draw on your readings for this lesson and on your own studies.

As you did with the aces and twos, come up with a single word that best expresses the meaning of each of the threes as you understand it. Commit these to memory.

As before, do at least four sessions of meditation during the two weeks you spend on this lesson. Feel free, however, to do more, up to as often as once each day. Any day in which you do not do a meditation, do the relaxation and attention drill given in lesson 3.

RITUAL

The Lesser Banishing Ritual of the Pentagram should be a part of your daily routine by this point. Continue to practice it each day. As you work with this rite over the next two weeks, put particular effort into tracing and visualizing the pentagrams and other imagery as clearly and exactly as possible. Try to build up the images so clearly in your imagination that they appear to be present even to your ordinary senses.

LESSON REVIEW

1. Perform the meditation or the attention exercise each day (see pages 94 and 51).
2. Perform the daily recollection each day on going to bed (see page 20).
3. Perform the Lesser Banishing Ritual of the Pentagram each day (see page 51).
4. Perform the reading exercise each day (see page 31).
5. Work on the number exercise described above over the next two weeks.
6. Perform the will exercise described above at least four times over the next two weeks.
7. Keep a record of your work.

When you have spent at least two weeks on these practices and have completed at least the minimum requirements listed above, you are ready to go on to lesson 7.

LESSON 7
THE MAGICAL LINK

Lessons 5 and 6 discussed some of the basic ways in which magicians of the Western tradition understand the universe around them, as well as the universe within them. These two worlds make up the field in which the magician operates, as they do the total range of resources available for the magician's work. Both these realms, as we have discussed, share a common structure that enables either to be interpreted in the other's terms.

This common structure has other implications for the magician, however. The relationship between the outer and inner universes opens up the possibility of linkages, in which potencies in one realm can connect with their equivalents in the other. Methods of creating such linkages have been, at times, among the more jealously guarded secrets of traditional magical orders, though many such secrets have become fairly common knowledge in the occult community in recent years.

The obsession with secret techniques, and with technique in general, tends to obscure the fact that these linkages (like every other element of practical magic) work because they imitate natural processes, processes that, quite literally, occur at every second in every human being. Careful attention to the ordinary events of aware-ness and of life, carried out patiently, will reveal the whole range of magical "secrets" to the observant student without any need for the blood-curdling oaths once commonly used in such contexts.

There is something to be said for a system of magical training that relies on just this approach. At the same time, such a system involves a fair amount of reinventing the wheel, and a certain danger to stu-dents whose personal imbalances are reflected in, and thereafter rein-forced by, the techniques they discover. Here, as elsewhere in esoteric work, a standard way of working has its uses, if only as a starting point for further personal exploration. It is in this spirit that the Middle Pillar exercise, one of the more effective means of opening up the link-ages referred to earlier, is presented a little later in this lesson.

EQUILIBRIUM AND THE BREAKING OF THE VESSELS

Our cosmos, according to an important Qabalistic tradition, was not the first cosmos created. There were others before it, but they failed, they collapsed in catastrophe. This collapse is explained in several ways, all of which point in a similar direction.

According to one explanation, the collapse came because equi-librium was never established: instead of opposing or complemen-tary forces, there were contending forces that were never moderated into harmonious mutual interaction.

Another refers to the structure and dynamics of the Tree of Life. If the Tree is seen as a fountain, with the divine creative impulse ever flowing from its superabundant source, then the sephiroth can be seen as basins of the fountain and the paths as pipes or spillways or aqueducts that channel the water from one basin to the next. If the ves-sels—either the basins or the channels—are not well designed, they will break, and the whole structure will be torn apart by the uncontained pressure of eternity striving to manifest in time. (In an important sense, however, the vessels were not set up before the flow began, but rather were created by and out of the flow itself.)

This series of primordial catastrophes account for one aspect of what we call evil. That is, evil is sometimes described as unbalanced force, acting without any internal or external equilibrium. Alternatively, evil is described as the shards and fragments of failed creations that still contain within them certain fragments of divine life. This is why one Qabalistic name for evil spirits is *qlippoth*, which can be translated as "shells" or "peelings." A similar image from northern European folklore is that of the tree spirits who seem beautiful and alluring as long as they don't turn around, but are in fact hollow and rotted husks, hungry for the souls of those they entice.

Our cosmos, then, was not built on virgin land. It was built on the rubble of several earlier unsuccessful construction projects, rubble that has become part of the foundation of our own cosmos. In the same way that rubble and landfill can cause unexpected problems for new structures, the fragments of these earlier attempts at creating a cosmos cause trouble for our cosmos, and for us.

Furthermore, the same kind of catastrophe is a constant possibility at any level of emerging manifestation in our own cosmos. Whenever something moves toward manifestation, there is always the possibility that something may go wrong: the forces may be, as it were, unbalanced, or the vessels may not be strong enough to contain the process.

The transition phases between one stage of life and another are a good example of this, as, on another level, is the learning of any skill. Although things generally go fairly well, there is always the possibility that something may go wrong and require a good deal of remedial work to put it right—to the extent that it can be put right. This is as true in social or educational or personal development as it is in biological development. Bad habits, once learned, can be quite difficult to unlearn, and this is as true of the spirit as it is of the body or mind.

Puberty is an example of a stage of life in which the level and kinds of energy at work increase. People react differently to this intensification of pressure and increased availability of energy. Some glory in it and spend it freely; some fight against it by establishing rigid control, or by trying to reduce it in one way or another.

The court cards of the tarot are emblems of different balanced combinations of energies or (in the old sense) "temperaments." Just as each element is a particular equilibrium of opposing qualities (hot/cold, wet/dry, a balance of opposites), each court card is an equilibrium of primary and secondary elements, or, in the language of the traditional Western art of healing, "humoral types." (The modern meaning of the word "humor" is a remnant of this older terminology: you are in good spirits, "good humor," when your humors or elemental factors are in balance.)

Each court card, however, also contains its own possibilities for imbalance, its own way of "running off the rails" when pressure is applied. Thus the King of Swords may slip into extreme harshness, while the Queen of Pentacles may be at risk of complete inertia. Attention to these potentials for imbalance can help you come to a clear knowledge of the ways you yourself may tend to slip into imbalance, and what pressures tend to bring this about.

READING

For this lesson, continue as before with your chosen book, reading the thirteenth and fourteenth chapters, selecting the seven sentences from each chapter that seem to you to express the chapter's most important points, and keeping company with one of the sentences on each day. As you begin working on this lesson, assess the results of your effort over the last two weeks to make use of the resources of your sleeping mind. This project may or may not have had any noticeable effects, and it may or may not have upset your sleep cycles to some degree or another. Assessing these points, decide whether you will continue to work on this for the next two weeks. Once you have decided, carry out your decision.

WILL EXERCISE

You have now had the opportunity to exercise both the dynamic and the static forms of the will using fairly simple practices. There are many other methods of training the will in the Hermetic magical tradition, ranging from exercises of the same degree of simplicity up to challenging disciplines requiring an enormous degree of commitment and effort.

Since this course is intended to be an introduction to Hermetic high magic, not an advanced course, the exercises presented here will remain toward the simpler end of the spectrum. Not all of the work we offer is as simple as the exercises already given, however, and later we will also discuss ways that will training can be integrated with the ordinary events of daily life.

The exercise for this lesson turns to a different aspect of the will. Instead of working with action and inaction, it works with attention and perception. Sitting in a comfortable position, turn your attention to your right hand. Do not look at it; feel it from within. Your goal is to perceive it as clearly, thoroughly, and exactly as possible, and to receive every message that the nerves in the hand are sending you.

Ignore every sensation that does not come from your hand. Maintain this concentration for five minutes.

During each day that you spend on this lesson, choose some part of your body and perceive it from within in this same way, letting the rest of the world fade from your awareness. Focus on a different body part each day. As always, write up the details of the experience in your magical journal.

NUMBER EXERCISE

Just as the first three sephiroth on the Tree of Life form the foundation of the Tree's entire structure, the first three numbers—in a sense, what the sephiroth of the Supernal Triad are at their root—are fundamental to the magical understanding of numbers in the Western esoteric tradition. Threefold patterns and rhythms occur as frequently in Western magical and esoteric teachings as they do in the legends and folklore of the world. Typically, just as in the Tree of Life, each triad is seen as giving rise to another through a cyclical process. In words attributed to Hermes Trismegistus, the legendary founder of alchemy and magic: "Out of the One comes the Two; out of the Two comes the Three; and out of the Three comes the One as the Fourth."

Thus, in one sense, each number after three can be seen as a repetition of one of the first three numbers: four becomes a second one, five a second two, and so on. In another sense, however, each of these numbers has its own significance and its own energy.

Your task for this exercise is to seek out this significance and energy for each of the numbers from four to ten, finding personal meanings for them just as you did for one, two, and three. You may take them in order, or work on them more or less all at once, as you prefer. Since this can be a fairly extensive task, we don't ask you to finish the whole process in two weeks! Your work on this number exercise will continue, along with the other work in these lessons, over the next several months; it should be completed, in at least some sense, by the time you reach lesson 15.

MEDITATION

During the last three lessons, the meditative side of your coursework has focused on developing a certain level of skill and familiarity with one basic form of this practice: discursive meditation on a visual symbol. By now, you have some experience with the way that your mind responds to this sort of work—an experience that is ultimately of much greater importance than anything you may have discovered about the subjects of the meditation.

The meditation for this lesson involves a slightly different focus. The framework of the practice (time, posture, opening and closing, relaxation, breathing, etc.) follows the pattern you've been using since lesson 3. Once you have completed the process of opening and are ready to begin meditating, however, instead of calling to mind an image, repeat inwardly the alchemical text given above:

Out of the One comes the Two; out of the Two comes t
he Three; and out of the Three comes the One as
the Fourth.

Your task in this meditation is to understand this sentence as completely as possible. Do not be satisfied with a single interpretation or a summary of the apparent meaning; the text can be read and applied in many ways. Feel free to draw on previous meditations, readings, or any other source for inspiration. One obvious (and entirely valid) direction lies in seeing the text as a discussion of the way the first three sephiroth interact.

If you find your mind wandering away from the topic, repeat the text inwardly and pick up where you left off. As before, ten minutes of actual meditation are enough for any one session; however, you should do at least six sessions of meditation on this topic during the two weeks you work on this lesson, and you are welcome to do more. Do the attention exercise on page 51 on any day you do not do a meditation.

TAROT EXERCISES

This lesson's work includes two exercises with the tarot deck. Each should be done at least once, and you can do either or both more than once if this seems useful. Each will take approximately half an hour.

1. Settle down in your practice space, get comfortable, and perform the opening gesture (see page 15).
2. Separate the court cards from the rest of your deck, and set the other cards aside.
3. Divide the court cards by suit and order them by rank: King-Queen-Knight-Page (or Knight-Queen-Prince-Princess, depending on the titles your deck uses).
4. Lay out the Wands royalty in order, left to right. Study each card in turn. The King represents the energies of elemental fire expressed through itself; the Queen, elemental water expressed through elemental fire; the Knight, elemental air expressed through elemental fire; the Page, elemental earth expressed through elemental fire.

5. Consider the modulating and altering effects on elemental fire of the four elements through which it is being channeled, and try to grasp something of the personality and approach to life characterized by this combination.

You need not rely on any of the traditional symbolism of the elements here; the everyday experiences of fire, water, air, and earth, which gave rise to the symbolism in the first place, are easily as useful in this context. For example, the combination of fire and fire is energetic but ill-fueled; the King of Wands may have enormous drive and energy, but may tend to lose interest abruptly and turn to other pursuits. Water coming through fire creates steam: flexible and adaptable, capable of doing much useful work, but also liable to explode if placed under too much pressure. Air with fire produces a steady flame: harmonious interaction, balanced energies, and a bright, relatively stable intellect. Earth expressed through fire engenders a practical focus for the ambitions natural to fire and grounds fire's volatile energies; it can be likened to banked embers, which, properly cared for, will preserve fire even under relatively adverse conditions.

These are examples of the kind of thinking needed for this exercise, not rigid forms that you need to observe and copy. Feel free to change them and depart from them to the extent that your own perceptions make this appropriate.

6. Note your observations about the Wands royalty, and return them to the deck.
7. Lay out the Cups royalty and study them in the same way: the four elements channeled through elemental water. Seek a feel for the difference between water-through-fire (the Queen of Wands) and fire-through-water (the King of Cups). Where

water acting within a context of fire may be seen as generating productive but also explosive steam, fire coming through water is largely doused, producing a tepid warmth of feeling and an amiable but rather detached nature. Pay attention, also, to the pure form of the element. Water through water is as unbalanced as fire and fire, but in different ways and with different results. Note your observations and return the Cups royalty to the deck.

8. Lay out the Swords court cards and continue as above. Note your observations and return the cards you have just studied to the deck.

9. Lay out the Pentacles royalty and continue. Write up your observations and make any final notes you wish before making the closing gesture.

This completes the first exercise. The second exercise takes about the same amount of time as the first, and follows similar lines.

1. Settle down in your practice space, make yourself comfortable, and perform the opening gesture (see page 15).

2. Separate the court cards out from the deck, and set the remaining cards aside.

3. Separate the court cards by rank, grouping the four kings, four queens, etc.

4. Lay out the four kings in suit order: Wands, Cups, Swords, Pentacles.

5. Study the different ways in which each king expresses the energies of fire. (In the first exercise, you examined the effects of the suit-element on the rank-element; now reverse the process.)

6. Note your observations and go on to study the four queens and water, the four knights and air, and the four pages and earth.

7. When you're finished, perform the closing gesture.

RITUAL: THE MIDDLE PILLAR EXERCISE

Two months' work on the Lesser Banishing Ritual of the Pentagram, has given you an opportunity to gain some sense of the way this basic ritual of Western magic operates. As with the basic meditative method already covered, a great deal of time—years, in fact—can be spent profitably on the study of this one ritual. Simple though it is, it contains a wealth of potentials and approaches that become apparent only through experience and intensive use.

At the same time, there are other aspects of basic ritual work that have a definite place in the elementary curriculum of Western esotericism. The exercise that follows is, perhaps, the most important of these.

Many spiritual traditions around the world conceptualize and construct systems of subtle energy centers within the human body. The number and position of these centers vary widely from system to system; certain martial arts–related disciplines operate with a single center in the belly, while some traditions of inner transformation make use of as many as 360 distinct centers located throughout and around the body.

The Western esoteric tradition has worked with several different systems of this kind through the years. In the specific branch of the tradition we teach, however, one system using five centers has become standard during the last century. These five centers correspond to the five levels of being we discussed in earlier lessons, as well as to the five elements and five aspects of the Tree of Life.

The following practice helps you awaken these centers and work with the energies that can be brought through them. It is the first phase of an exercise that will be developed in more detail later.

1. Perform the complete Lesser Banishing Ritual of the Pentagram as before, beginning and ending with the Qabalistic Cross (see page 38).

2. Standing in the center of the banished space facing east, direct your attention to an imagined point of light far above your head.

3. Breathe in and, as you do so, visualize a beam of intense white light descending from that point. This beam stops just above the top of your head and there forms a sphere of brilliant white about six inches across. (This sphere should not quite touch your scalp.) Hold this image with as much clarity as possible for a time, and then vibrate the divine name *AHIH* ("Eh-heh-yeh").

4. With another inhalation, visualize the beam of light descending from the sphere above your head to a point in the center of your throat. There it forms another sphere of light of the same size and color. Hold this image for approximately the same amount of time as the first, and then vibrate the divine name *YHVH ALHIM* ("Ye-ho-wah Ell-oh-heem").

5. Repeat the process, bringing the beam of light down to your heart with another inhalation and forming another sphere of white light there. After you have held this image for the same amount of time, vibrate the name *YHVH ALVH VDAaTh* ("Ye-ho-wah Ell-oh-ah Vah Da-at").

6. Repeat the process, establishing a sphere of light in your genital area. Vibrate the name *ShDI AL ChI* ("Shah-dai Ell Chai," with the "ch" a hard sound as in "Bach" or "Loch Ness").

7. Repeat the process, establishing a sphere of light beneath the soles of your feet. Vibrate the name *ADNI HARTz* ("Ah-doh-nai Ha Ah-retz").

8. Pause, and visualize as intensely as possible all five of the centers and the beam of light linking them together.

9. Perform the Qabalistic Cross once more to complete the exercise.

Do this exercise once each day, preferably at the same time. This includes and replaces the daily pentagram ritual you have been doing.

LESSON REVIEW

1. Perform the meditation or attention exercise each day (see pages 103 and 51).

2. Perform the daily recollection each day on going to bed (see page 20).

3. Perform the will exercise described above each day.

4. Perform the reading exercise described above each day.

5. Practice the Middle Pillar exercise described above daily.

6. Do each of the tarot exercises described above at least once.

7. Begin work on the number exercise described above.

8. Keep a record of your work.

When you have worked at these exercises for at least two weeks and have completed at least the minimum requirements given above, you are ready to proceed to lesson 8.

LESSON 8

KNOW
YOURSELF

Above the gateway of the great oracular shrine at Delphi, perhaps
the holiest place in ancient Greece, were carved the words *Gnothi
seauton*—"Know yourself." From the standpoint of magical tradition, this inscription stands atop the gateway to every kind of magical and spiritual attainment. This complex structure we each call "I"
is the primary tool of magic, as it is of every other pursuit in life. Its
potentials and powers—not all of them obvious—need to be understood if they are to be developed and used.

A significant part of this self-knowledge is wordless and incom-
municable, and can be learned only through experience and introspection. Another part, however, is somewhat less evasive. Many
traditions contain the idea of multiple levels of meaning, which can
be seen as an intellectual equivalent of the idea of multiple worlds.
Just as there are various worlds—from the physical through the etheric
and astral, to the spiritual—there are different worlds of meaning. A
story like *Through the Looking Glass* can thus have a literal meaning,
a psychological meaning, a political or social meaning, perhaps a

scientific or alchemical meaning, a doctrinal meaning, and a spiritual meaning.

A common practice in the Middle Ages was to read four kinds of meaning from Biblical texts: a literal or historical one, an allegorical one, a psychological one, and a spiritual or mystical one. This was not an innovation, but a kind of systematization of the multiple readings of the ancient world, in which Homer could be read as psychology, natural science, or philosophy. A fourfold interpretation was also used in Jewish tradition, with the fourth, "secret," level being the Qabalah itself. These four were summarized in the acronym PRDS, which spells the word *pardes,* or "garden." The four levels are literal, allegorical, ethical, and secret: *peshat, remez, derash,* and *sod.* Needless to say, these are only categories. Within each category, numberless specific intepretations are possible.

These levels of interpretation are primarily pointers to different ways of analyzing or understanding. It is one thing to understand literally, another to understand allegorically, another to understand ethically or psychotherapeutically, and yet another to understand spiritually or mystically. It is a useful exercise in discursive meditation to examine any subject from all four perspectives. It is also useful to develop one or more schemes of interpretation (for example, a scheme with three levels, one with five levels, and one with seven levels) and to apply them in discursive meditation in turn.

The injunction, "Know yourself," can be taken literally, even materially, by making an objective catalogue of your own traits. It can also be taken ethically, by becoming familiar with your mind and character as they are—not shying away from the unpleasant or being complacent about the pleasant, but keeping an eye to more effective self-management. There is, however, a third way it can be taken: as an injunction to know who is knowing—that is, to know your own consciousness directly and fully.

In the first mode, you know yourself as a collection of traits; there is a sharp distinction between subject and object, the knower and what is known. In the second, you know yourself as you struggle with your own habits; there is less distinction between subject and object. In the third, what is known is not an object of knowledge; rather, attention attends to itself. This is sometimes called "seeing as we are seen," the idea being to collapse the distinction between the one who sees and the one who is seen. The knowledge is a direct recognition that there is no "self" to be grasped as an object, but a welling up from the springs of the unmanifest that differentiates into subject and object. At its source, it is neither, but you may find that it is some primal act through which your existence is uttered into manifestation.

The Western magical traditions contain a great deal of material on the nature and structure of the human microcosm, tracing out the details of an "anatomy" that does not stop at the borders of matter. Part of this material, dealing with different levels of the self, has already been covered in this course. Interacting with these levels, however, is a series of structures or functions of the self. These relate to the levels as given earlier, but in places the fit is not exact; there are overlaps and interconnections not obvious at first glance. And it is very important to remember that, although they can be drawn in a two-dimensional diagram or laid out in a table, these labels and diagrams should not be taken too literally.

On the more external levels, there are indeed structures that can be known as objects, the way an anatomist knows nerves and muscles. But an anatomist is not a lover, and the lover's way of knowing nerves and muscles is a different and more inward kind of knowledge, in which the structures are not known as objects, but rather through and as a means of experience. The higher or more inward the level, the less polarization there is: at the highest or most inward, to know yourself is to know your own experience to its root as it blossoms from moment to moment at the intersection of any particular place and time. This kind of self-knowledge is very evasive, because people are so accustomed to working with a strong polarization between subject and object. The kind of knowing for which diagrams and tables are the vehicle is much more familiar. Properly approached, however, this sort of knowledge can be a very helpful tool in guiding the seeker to the higher, unpolarized knowing.

The physical body, called the *guph* by Qabalists, corresponds closely to the material level of existence discussed earlier. Similarly, the vital body, called the *nephesh*, corresponds to the etheric level, although there is some overlap. The nephesh reaches into subtler aspects of the physical body, affecting, among other things, the endocrine glands. On the Tree of Life, these two correspond to Malkuth and Yesod, respectively.

It is with the next level, the *ruach*, or personality, that things become more complicated. The ruach includes the astral level of concrete consciousness, and to some extent—an extent that varies from person to person depending on the state of inner development—the mental level of abstract consciousness as well. The five aspects of ordinary human consciousness (intellect, emotion, imagination, will, and memory) are assigned to the ruach and correspond to the five sephiroth Hod, Netzach, Tiphareth, Geburah, and Chesed, in that order. (These five aspects are not quite all on the same level; as we will show later, some are present in ordinary human consciousness in a more direct sense than are others. For the time being, however, the difference is not of great importance.)

Above the ruach, in the place of the Supernal Triad, are the three spiritual aspects of the self: the *neshamah*, or spiritual understanding, corresponding to Binah; the *chiah*, or spiritual will, corresponding to Chokmah; and the *yechidah*, or essential spiritual being, corresponding to Kether. These three form the spiritual self, and the one term *neshamah* is used for all.

To some extent, this classification can be understood as merely another set of correspondences to the Tree of Life, to be used in meditation and study as you might use the astrological correspondences. Here, however, further potentials exist as well. In the work of self-knowledge, it can be highly useful to sort out different parts of the self, to recognize the source or location of problems or issues, and to identify factors involved in inner conflicts. In such situations, this sort of anatomy of the self is as useful—indeed, as necessary—as ordinary anatomy is to a physician. For this reason, you should become familiar with the classification given here, and explore the ways in which it relates to your own experience of yourself.

THEORY, ORDER, CORRESPONDENCE: CHESED

Theory has a rather problematic place in esotericism. Sometimes it seems, especially to people who look at esotericism from the outside, that theory is the only point of esotericism. An "occultist," in fact, is generally taken to be someone committed to a theory of the world that is profoundly contrary both to science and common sense. Some kinds of esoteric thought do make claims about what kind of world we live in, claims that can be examined in the same way that scientific or philosophical claims can be. Important aspects of esoteric theory, however, are more akin to music theory: less about what is the case, and more about how to achieve certain results. Like music theory, this sort of theory has a double effect: it makes results possible, but it also limits the results that can be achieved.

Someone who encounters esoteric theory for the first time often misunderstands its purpose. One good example is the theory of correspondences, which seems like a highly implausible set of claims about the world until you begin to see how it is used. That the Sun "corresponds" to gold, for example, makes at best an arbitrary and conventional sense, until you begin to see that the statement must be interpreted to mean something more like "the Sun, among the traditional planets, is like gold among the metals." This is one reason why the same thing has different correspondences depending on context.

Just as sets of objects correspond to other sets of objects, processes correspond to other processes. Thus, among the elements, fire can be taken as the initiating spark, and water the reflective, sustaining reaction or response. Their interaction generates vapor, the balance of the two—that is, air. The three then stabilize into a solid triangular structure, the stable unity of earth, which paradoxically can also serve as the fiery spark initiating a new development. Alternatively, a cycle can be taken to start with air, the tentative hints of dawn, and progress through the fire of noon and the fluidity of dusk into the deep, solid obscurity of midnight. Neither of these structures is exclusively true; either can serve as the key to other correspondences.

In certain states of delusion or delirium, the deep roots of the theory of correspondences in the human mind become very clear. Many people have had the experience of seeing something in a dream and immediately knowing what it represents and how it fits into the ongoing dream. Something similar happens in delirium, when a hallucination, triggered by some stimulus, carries with it a complete organizing story that overlays and overrides other perceptions. Thus, someone may see the form of someone who died long ago and have a long conversation with that form without any surprise or sense of incongruity, losing track of surroundings in the course of responding to the field of associations that has crystallized around one perceived form. Many experiences, especially meditative or magical experiences, are like emblems or icons. They are perceived as a whole, perhaps in a flash, and decoded gradually through a process of examination and attention. This is one reason that work with the tarot keys is so valuable for students of magic.

When correspondences and their key structures have been assimilated, they achieve a certain autonomy. They begin to speak for themselves, in effect, and to provide intuitive keys to a vast range of situations. There are times when certain correspondences, or rather their structures or formulas, can come alive for those who have assimilated them, so that they become aware of them not as objects of thought, but as centers of conscious thought in their own right.

This is one of the modes of what is sometime called "inner-plane communication"—a contact with abstract structures that are experienced directly as having a life, an inwardness, of their own. It is this kind of experience that is indicated, in another context, when older books of occultism speak of direct, abstract, mind-to-mind contact with "the Masters."

Theories about Masters can be understood as attempts to understand certain kinds of meditative or magical experience. In meditation, or in other forms of magical work, what may in one mode of consciousness seem like an abstract idea or an impersonal energy, can seem instead like an entity with its own center of awareness or its own vitality. Without theory, it would be very difficult to recognize and work with such subtle and abstract realms of experience. At the same time, the theory, even when enlivened by experience, cannot simply be taken literally and concretely. Such literal, concrete interpretations

of esoteric theory can easily lead to bigotry, self-righteous imposi-
tions on others, and a blindness to seeing that a particular structure
may be very useful in one situation without being universally true —
or requiring one to enforce universal agreement.

In traditional terms, the grade of inner development that corresponds to Chesed is named *Adeptus Exemptus*, "exempt adept." The
"exemption" of the exempt adepts consists, at least in part, in this: that
they are not dominated by any one of the structures with which they
work, since they do not mistake such structures as the ultimate sources
or springs of meaning. Their gaze is directed farther and deeper, toward
that from which these great abstract energies derive their being.

SYMBOLISM OF CHESED

As part of this lesson's work, you will learn a selection of the symbols attributed to the fourth sephirah, Chesed, Mercy. These are as
follows:

Divine name: AL (pronounced "Ell")

Archangel: Tzadkiel, "Justice of God"

Angelic order: Chashmalim, "Brilliant Ones"

Astrological correspondence: Tzedek, the planet Jupiter

Tarot correspondence: the four fours of the deck

As before, commit these correspondences to memory, and write
the second, third, fourth, and fifth onto your Tree of Life diagram
in the four circles of Chesed. Then color the remainder of the sephirah blue.

THE NINETEENTH, TWENTIETH, AND TWENTY-FIRST PATHS

As in previous lessons, you must learn a selection of symbols relating to the paths that extend from Chesed to other sephiroth on the Tree of Life. While the detailed theory of the paths is not something an introductory course of this sort can or should cover, it is worth noting that the paths that lead from any sephirah further down the Tree can be understood as expressions of the sephirah's energy and nature. It may be instructive to think of the paths you have already learned, and those covered here, in this context.

The paths and symbols for the two weeks you spend on this lesson are as follows:

Nineteenth path

Position on the Tree: Chesed to Geburah

Hebrew letter: ט, Teth

Tarot correspondence: Trump VIII, Strength

Astrological correspondence: Leo

Twentieth path

Position on the Tree: Chesed to Tiphareth

Hebrew letter: י, Yod

Tarot correspondence: Trump IX, the Hermit

Astrological correspondence: Virgo

Twenty-first path

Position on the Tree: Chesed to Netzach

Hebrew letter: כ, Kaph

Tarot correspondence: Trump X, the Wheel of Fortune

Astrological correspondence: Jupiter

As before, commit these to memory and rehearse them with the aid of the corresponding tarot trumps.

READING

The reading exercise for this lesson follows the same lines as those for previous lessons. Read one chapter from your chosen book each week, select the seven sentences that seem to express the chapter's most important ideas, and keep company with one of those sentences on each day of the following week.

You have probably found already that there are some times that this exercise seems interesting, and other times that it requires a great deal of effort. Pay attention to variations of this sort. What, if anything, seems to make the difference between one and the other?

SELF-PERCEPTION EXERCISE

A certain type of knowledge about the self, as we mentioned above, can be attained through the study of theoretical material on the various structures and functions of the human being. Another type, of course, cannot. No amount of Qabalistic theory will enable you to perceive the particular strengths and weaknesses, the particular stresses and interplays between levels, that make you who you are. (The theory may help you understand what you are perceiving, but that is a different matter.)

One part of the work facing any student of the Western mysteries, then, is simple introspection: the act of paying attention to the self, of learning to notice what is happening on the nearer side of the boundary between "I" and everything else.

To call introspection "simple," however, is to indulge in a half-truth. As with so many other things in esoteric work, it is simple in theory, but annoyingly complex in practice. Many of the same difficulties that beset the would-be meditator interfere with self-perception as well, and for many of the same reasons. It is rarely sufficient to do as some schools have done and simply tell students to be aware of themselves!

The following exercise will help you explore some of the issues involved in self-perception. Set aside at least an hour when you will not be disturbed, and provide yourself with plenty of paper and a pen or pencil, since the exercise consists of making four lists.

1. Make a list of your proven strengths—that is, the things that you know you can do well because you have actually done them well, in a context in which the quality of your efforts has been tested and proved.

2. Make a list of your potential strengths—that is, the things you think you can probably do well, but that you have not yet put to the test, or not yet developed through the necessary training and experience.

3. Make a list of your proven weaknesses—that is, those things you know you do not handle well, because you have actually experienced failure or awkwardness in attempting them.

4. Make a list of your potential weaknesses—that is, those things which you suspect you would not do well, but which you have never attempted.

Be careful not to turn this exercise into an opportunity either to bask in the glow of your ego or to berate yourself for assorted failings. If your list becomes overloaded on either side of the ledger, stop for a moment and work at restoring a sense of perspective. Your task is to assess yourself without passing moral judgment—a difficult job for many people, but one with enormous benefits.

Equally, be sure that you are not neglecting any significant side of yourself. Go through your lists with the structure of your self in mind, exploring your strengths and weaknesses on all levels—physical, mental, etheric, astral, and spiritual. You can also check your lists using the four functions of intellect, emotion, intuition, and sensation.

When you have finished the lists, put them away in a secure place. Go back to them several days later and review them, making any appropriate changes. Make notes on the experience and the feelings it arouses in you in your magical journal.

THE ART OF MEMORY

As mentioned earlier, the process and faculty of memory is both one of the correspondences of Chesed and the highest of the five aspects of the ruach, the ordinary human consciousness. It may seem strange that memory was given so important a place; current theories and practices of education have taught many modern people to despise "rote memorization" and to replace it wherever possible with artificial aids.

Memory, however, is quite literally the means by which each of us constructs the world in which we live. At any given moment, only a minute fraction of that world is perceptible to us by any other means. To the extent that we take anything outside of that fraction into account in our thoughts or actions, we are relying on memory. Furthermore, the meanings and significances of things in that world, perceived at the moment or not, are all held in and founded on memory.

In earlier times, considerations such as these—as well as the real advantages of a good memory in an age before public libraries and computer databases—led to the creation of systems of memory training. Ultimately, several of the most effective of these were combined and adapted by magicians into a system of inner work, the Art of Memory, in which a thoroughly trained memory became a vessel for transformative powers.

Such a system is well beyond the scope of this introductory course. A simpler version of it, however, can be useful both practically and as a magical discipline. Follow these simple steps:

1. Choose a room or other space that you know well. Books on the Art of Memory advise using open, relatively uncluttered spaces with five to ten distinct "places" where objects can be put. This is good advice to follow.
2. Take the time to walk through the space, physically and also in your imagination, until you can readily and quickly call it to mind in your mind's eye. Pay particular attention to the places in your space.
3. When you have a number of things you wish to remember— for example, a grocery list—take the first item on the list and imagine it in the first place in your visualized space. Make the image as clear and solid as possible.

4. Go on to the second item on the list, put it in the second place, and repeat the process until you have finished the list or run out of places.

5. When you need to remember the list, mentally go through the space again, looking at each of the places as you come to it. You will find the images you put there, each one in its place.

It's best to start with short lists and work up gradually to long ones, and of course practice makes perfect here as elsewhere. Art of Memory textbooks advise you to make the images striking in some way, so that your memory retains them more easily. Here, the personal element is central; some people find humorous or bizarre images most effective, others do not. Experiment until you find the sort of image that sticks best in your mind.

With practice, the construction of these images becomes both quick and easy. You will find that the images you use for memory purposes do not remain after they are no longer needed; you needn't worry about a grocery list showing up at some later date when the same space is holding dates for a history test!

Your assignment for this part of the work is to use the basic Art of Memory given here at least four times during the next two weeks. The more often you use it and the longer you continue to use it, the more prepared you will be for more advanced forms of the Art of Memory.

MEDITATION

For this lesson's meditative work, we will return to the form and format introduced in lesson 4. For the next two weeks, the topic for your meditations is the four fours of the tarot. As the expressions of

Chesed through the four elements and Four Worlds, these cards have much to teach about the essential ordering principles of the Western esoteric tradition. As before, work with one card in each session of meditation, and feel free to draw on this lesson's reading assignment and your other studies.

Here, as with your earlier meditative work with the tarot, come up with a single word that best expresses the meaning of each of the cards and commit them to memory.

Plan on doing at least eight sessions of meditation during the two weeks you spend on this lesson. As before, every day in which you do not do a meditation, do the relaxation and attention exercises given in lesson 3.

RİTUAL

Perform the Middle Pillar exercise (see page 107) each day during the time you spend on this lesson. As you work with this rite over the next two weeks, review the instructions in lesson 7 frequently, and concentrate on making the visualizations as clear and exact as possible.

LESSOΠ REVİEW

1. Perform the meditation or attention exercise each day (see pages 124 and 51).
2. Perform the daily recollection each day on going to bed (see page 20).
3. Perform the Middle Pillar exercise each day (see page 107).
4. Perform the reading exercise every day (see page 31).
5. Use the Art of Memory exercise described above at least four times over the next two weeks.

6. Perform the self-perception exercise described above each day.
7. Continue working on the number exercise presented in lesson 7.
8. Keep a record of your work.

When you have spent at least two weeks on these practices and have completed at least the minimum required work, you are ready to go on to lesson 9.

LESSON 9

THE DIMENSIONS
OF WILL

The Tree of Life has become one of the core tools of Western esotericism because of its wide applicability. It is not, of course, as a diagram on a piece of paper, or even as a diagram generated by a specific
method of construction, that it is so widely applicable. It is as a diagram that has come to be used in a very particular way.

Beginning students of Latin are asked to read selected passages
from certain standard authors—from Caesar's *Gallic Wars*, for example, or from Virgil's *Aeneid*. By learning the language through studying a standard text, they learn much more than what is in the text, or
the basic rules of the language. They learn, by example, how texts
are written in that language and how they are read.

In very much the same way, by working with the Tree, by unpack-
ing layer after layer of information, and mode after mode of gaining
access to that information, you learn more than just vast tables of
correspondences. You learn to perform the kinds of activities that
lead you to contact the realms of living experience of which those
correspondences are the outer and visible signs. The point, after all,
of reading Virgil is not to learn the rules of Latin grammar and poetry

for their own sake, but for the sake of the ability they give you, when you have made them your own, to experience Virgil's poetry. Likewise, when you work with the Tree, you learn to experience the realms for which it provides a coordinate system.

VIRTUES AND VICES

One very important use to which the Tree can be put is to increase self-knowledge, and one of the most important tasks for any aspirant to esoteric training is to come to know yourself. This is one of the ways in which magical training parts ways with modern education. Magical tradition has not the slightest interest in so-called "self-esteem," in providing, maintaining, or protecting a positive self-image—or a negative one, or any particular image at all. The point of esoteric training is to learn to see what is there to be seen, and not to flinch, slide, shiver, tap-dance, or otherwise turn away from it in favor of some secondary representation or comfortable substitute.

On the most basic, down-home level, this means you have to practice seeing yourself clearly—and this, in turn, means you have to learn to discern your own virtues and vices. But before you can do that, you have to learn to recognize what virtues and vices are. And this is where the Tree is a very great help indeed.

The correspondences given for the sephiroth in standard textbooks on the subject include, among many other things, virtues and vices. These listings of specific actions and qualities can be seen as the first, shallowest aspect of the Tree's analysis: a somewhat arbitrary set of characteristics assigned to the sephiroth according to the usual symbolic scheme. This corresponds, in many ways, to the rule-following morality common to most established religions.

Within the bare lists, however, is a deeper governing principle. Consider three responses to a threat of lethal violence—a belligerent drunk looking for trouble with a knife in his hand, for instance. One response is to pull out a revolver and pump the man full of lead from ten yards. Another is to cringe in the shadows hoping not to be seen, and hurry away as quickly as possible trying to ignore the screams of some poor innocent not as good at hiding. A third is to face the man and, in one way or another, use an appropriate level of force to disarm him—for example, taking advantage of the effects of alcohol on his reactions, trap his knife arm with a painful but nonlethal jujutsu hold, and pin him to the ground with a joint lock until the police can arrive.

All three of these responses (and, of course, the situation itself) have to do with the part of life the Qabalah assigns to Geburah. The first response goes too far in the direction of Geburah, while the second does not go far enough; both cruelty and cowardice are, in their own way, extremes. Between them, expressing Geburah in an appropriate manner, is the third response: courage. Similarly, most other vices can best be seen, not as the opposite of a virtue, but as the opposite of another vice, with a virtue as a third factor in between.

The characteristic of the third response can be called harmony, or appropriateness; most modern Qabalistic writings use the term "balance." Easier to experience than to define, harmony serves as the central theme of the magical approach to morality. It is the Middle Pillar upon the Tree of Life, as well as the middle path between extremes. Classical philosophers called this quality *sophrosyne*, often translated "temperance," though it may be significant that no English word provides an entirely satisfactory translation.

This third alternative has one other characteristic: it often requires skill or specialized training. It takes far less knowledge and ability to empty a gun into a hypothetical drunk or to hide behind a dumpster than to disarm him in hand-to-hand combat. Respect for technical ability has thus been common in magical circles for many centuries.

WILL: GEBURAH

Although it's not as fashionable as it once was, "will power" is mentioned in many writings on magical and occult subjects. The word itself has a rather old-fashioned sound today. This is not entirely unfortunate, although it is also partly due to the general abdication of responsibility characteristic of certain aspects of contemporary life.

Will is one of the four powers or magical virtues of the Sphinx—to know, to will, to dare, and to keep silent. These were codified by the magical theorist Eliphas Levi in the 19th century (on the pattern, most likely, of the four traditional "natural virtues" of courage, justice, temperance, and prudence). A trained and developed will is essential to the magician—as, in fact, it is to the mystic. The idea of a trained and developed will, however, almost immediately gives rise to the notion of "will power," either in the Victorian sense of clench-jawed rigidity, or in the related idea of a towering, turgid sense of dominating power and intensity that aims at its object to cow it into submission.

Neither of these is particularly near the mark. The truly effective will involves no strain or turbulence: it is quiet, relaxed, and inevitable. Indeed, the operation of the will only intrudes on awareness when the will is ineffective or impeded.

What is will, then, and how is it trained?

Will is simply a matter of what some schools of philosophy call intention, or intentionality. It is operative in every moment of consciousness, perception, and activity. There is a popular saying that, when the only tool you have is a hammer, every problem looks like a nail. The hammer here is any specific intent. Once it is set, everything else is organized around, or by, it in a way that makes sense in terms of the framework in which it has been set. If you are a private in an army, you see your environment in terms of orders to be obeyed (or avoided); if you are a general, you see your environment in terms of ways of exercising command. If you intend to play chess, a bit of flat ground and a set of pebbles can be a chess set; if you intend to play checkers, the same objects may, in that moment of intention, become a checkerboard with checker pieces.

The "strength" of this sort of will comes not from any process of pumping up but from clarity. You have to be clear about what a chess set is before you can take some set of objects as a chess set. The strength of the will derives from simplicity or unity of focus. If you can't decide whether to play chess or checkers, the patch of ground and pile of pebbles will not become either a chess or a checker set. It relies on unity or clarity of desire. If you want to play chess, but know your partner wants to play checkers, and you want to please your partner as well, it's anyone's guess as to whether the pile of pebbles will become checkers or chessmen.

Will, in its highest sense, is associated not so much with Geburah as with Kether. Geburah has a special connection with the exercise of will, however, since this sephirah is, above all, the sphere of discipline and correction. The root of all real power is power over yourself—self-mastery. The magical weapons or working tools traditionally assigned to Geburah provide a strong indication of this. To wield a spear or sword with much success takes practice, and this is true of other kinds of mastery as well. Asceticism, unfashionable though it may be, is not (as some see it today) an indulgence in self-destruction or craven self-denial. *Ascesis* is, literally, "training"—the training of the athlete. An ascetic is someone who is in training, thus ascesis is the root of power in several senses.

Asceticism is, in many times and places, a source of power simply because an ascetic is charismatic. To see someone who passes up pleasures that dominate others often produces a sense of awe, even if it is only the kind of amazement that people feel when they see someone perform a difficult or dangerous act. It is also a source of power because it provides independence from distracting desires. That in turn gives the ascetic the time and resources to devote to mastering other skills.

Asceticism is dedication in action, putting aside all that prevents you from reaching a goal, and working unceasingly at all that leads to its completion. Finally, asceticism is the discipline of emptying yourself of all that is meaningless in order to embody your vision of meaning. And this is why Geburah is linked with the imagery of the rose, which blooms on brambles—or in other symbolism on a cross— and why the sphere of Geburah is linked with the number 5, which the Pythagoreans took as the number of marriage.

SYMBOLISM OF GEBURAH

As part of this lesson's work, you will learn a selection of the symbols traditionally assigned to the fifth sephirah. These are as follows:

Divine name: ALHIM GBVR (pronounced "El-oh-heem Geh-boor")

Archangel: Kamael, "He who sees God"

Angelic order: Seraphim, "Fiery Ones"

Astrological correspondence: Madim, the planet Mars

Tarot correspondence: the four fives of the deck

As before, commit these correspondences to memory and write the first four into the four circles of Geburah on your Tree of Life diagram. Then color the rest of Geburah red.

The Twenty-Second and Twenty-Third Paths

You will also learn the basic symbolism of the two paths that extend down the Tree from Geburah; commit them to memory and use the corresponding tarot trumps to help with the learning process. The relevant paths and symbolism are as follows:

Twenty-second path

Position on the Tree: Geburah to Tiphareth

Hebrew letter: ל, Lamed

Tarot correspondence: Trump XI, Justice

Astrological correspondence: Libra

Twenty-third path

Position on the Tree: Geburah to Hod

Hebrew letter: מ, Mem

Tarot correspondence: Trump XII, the Hanged Man

Astrological correspondence: the element of Water

READING

While working on this lesson, continue with your reading exercise as described and discussed earlier. Put particular attention into bringing the daily sentence to your mind whenever you are standing in line, stuck in traffic, or otherwise forced to waste time. You are likely to find some degree—possibly a very high degree—of internal resistance to the act of keeping your thoughts centered on the sentence you have chosen. Observe this, and ask yourself what it is that you would rather be thinking about during these times.

TRANSMUTATION OF THE SELF

One of the things represented by Geburah in Qabalistic thought is the human will. This aspect of human consciousness comes in for a good deal of misunderstanding in our present culture. Too often, "will power" is associated with notions of white knuckles and internal conflict, or of some mental equivalent of the bulging muscles of bodybuilders. In fact, all of this is quite beside the point. Inner conflict and strain arise not from strength of will but from its weakness—or, more precisely, its division. When the will is unified, when all the different aspects of the self seek the same goal in the same way, that goal can be reached without the sort of fuss and difficulty encountered by the "strong-willed."

Obviously, then, attaining this unity of will is something well worth seeking, in ordinary life as well as in esoteric matters. At the same time, this quest has a certain circularity to it. How can you attain the unity of will to effectively seek unity of will? This problem may seem like little more than a word game, but difficulties like this are, in fact, the reasons behind most of the complicated methods of the esoteric path.

The following exercise helps you explore some of the subtler issues surrounding will. Use it to continue your training—a training that has been going on since the beginning of this course, in and out of the will exercises we have presented—in the unity of intention we have been discussing. At the same time, it introduces a simple but effective technique of practical magic, one that is particularly useful for the transmutation and balancing of undeveloped or undesired aspects of the personality.

1. Review the results of the self-perception exercise from lesson 8 (see page 120). Using these as a starting point, think about yourself—your strengths and weaknesses, the parts of yourself with which you are relatively satisfied and those that trouble you.

2. Either in your mind or, if you find this useful, on paper, take a rough inventory of yourself. This is intended to be a first approximation, not a final assessment.

3. When you have completed this, take some time to choose a part of your personality you feel "needs work"—either an overdeveloped aspect that you want to diminish, or an underdeveloped one you want to expand. Consider your choice carefully. One other point is important: don't let anyone else know just what part of your personality you've decided to address. Failure to observe this stricture will most likely make the exercise ineffective by bringing the interfering factor of another's will into the picture.

4. Do not choose an addiction you want to conquer as the focus of this exercise, at least for now. Most addicts have tried and failed to break the addictive cycle in the past, and this creates a habit of failure and an automatic division of will that can easily frustrate an inexperienced practitioner. The same applies, even

more strongly, to issues surrounding body weight, since natural processes in the metabolism make dieting and other supposed weight-loss methods self-defeating, except in the short term, for most people.

5. Think about the aspect of your personality you've chosen in the context of the four elements and their symbolism. Does it seem to be a thing of fire, of water, of air, or of earth? It may well overlap into several elements; still, choose the one that seems most appropriate.

6. Choose a tarot ace appropriate to the work you are setting out to do. If you have chosen to expand an underdeveloped part of your personality, choose the ace corresponding to that aspect's element; if you wish to decrease an overdeveloped aspect, choose the ace of the opposite element. (Fire and water are opposites, as are earth and air.)

7. Every morning upon rising for the next two weeks, take the ace you have chosen from the deck, sit in the usual position, and perform the opening gesture (see page 15).

8. Think briefly about the aspect of your personality you have chosen for this work, then let that fade and simply focus on the card. As far as possible, keep your mind entirely on the card for the duration of the exercise, which should be at least five minutes.

9. When you are finished, do the closing gesture and put the card away. During the two-week period, make no special effort to change your thoughts or behavior, or for that matter to keep these the same as they have been.

At the end of the two weeks, discontinue the practice, and assess any changes you may notice. Write a full description in your practice record.

WILL EXERCISE

Will is, in many ways, the central theme of this lesson, though all of the exercises presented in the course apply to it in one way or another. (This is particularly true of such standard, general magical exercises as meditation and the Middle Pillar exercise, since the sheer act of practicing any exercise every day is one of the classic ways to train will in the magical tradition.) Still, it is useful to continue the sequence of will exercises begun earlier at this point.

In essence, the exercise in this lesson is a more complex version of the first will exercise introduced back in lesson 4. For it, choose a place you have never been. It need not be particularly far away, but it should be unfamiliar. Locate it on a map and figure out where it is in relation to the places where you ordinarily spend time.

Having chosen the place, decide on a date and time to arrive there. It should be within the limits of possibility for you—for example, don't choose a date and time when you are supposed to be at work, unless you're willing to take time off for this exercise! Then, having settled place, date, and time, be there on time. There should be no reason for the trip other than the exercise.

Do this at least twice during the two weeks you spend on this lesson. As always, write up your experiences in your magical journal.

MEDITATION

For this lesson's meditative work, continue with the method of symbolic meditation introduced in lesson 4. For the next two weeks, your topics for work are the four fives of the tarot deck. As the expression of Geburah through the four elements and Four Worlds, these have much to teach about the esoteric understanding of energy and of transformation, in the universe as well as in the self. Work with one card in each meditation session, and draw on your readings and other studies as you see fit.

As before, come up with a single word to best express the meaning of each card as you understand it, then commit these words to memory.

Plan on doing at least eight sessions of meditation during the next two weeks. As before, on any day you do not meditate, do the relaxation and attention drill given in lesson 3.

RITUAL

Perform the Middle Pillar exercise (see lesson 7) each day during the two weeks you spend on this lesson. As you work with this ritual, concentrate on being aware of any changes in feeling or energy, either in yourself or in your practice space, during and after the rite.

LESSON REVIEW

1. Perform the meditation or attention exercise every day (see pages 137 and 51).
2. Perform the daily recollection each day upon going to bed (see page 20).
3. Perform the Middle Pillar exercise each day (see page 107).
4. Perform the reading exercise each day (see page 31).
5. Perform the will exercise described above at least twice during the two weeks you spend on this lesson.
6. Perform the transmutation exercise described above each morning on rising.
7. Continue working on the number exercise given in lesson 7.
8. Keep a record of your work.

When you have spent at least two weeks on these exercises and completed at least the minimum work listed above, you are ready to begin lesson 10.

LESSON 10

THE MIRROR
OF MOTIVES

In certain traditional magical orders, candidates for initiation are asked at some point in the ceremony why they want to enter the path of occult knowledge. The proper answer is: "I desire to know in order to serve." Often, however, candidates are prompted to give the response, and the implication of the rite becomes lost in a veil of nested ironies.

It is true that you must inevitably serve something—if not a sense of justice, or a delight in beauty and dislike for bad taste, then at least the needs of your belly or your fear of pain or discomfort. And it is also true that trying to serve two masters leaves you pretty much unable to follow either one.

The intention of the ritual question is clear enough. It teaches, by implication, that it is dedication—coherent service to some ideal or at least some goal—that opens the door to deeper awareness, and that it is a complete and integrated dedication to serving a certain kind of goal that leads to the deepest transmutations of your life and very being. But the very ritual circumstances also point out that it is very unlikely that a candidate will already have any spontaneous tendency to understand this point. In ritual terms, at any rate, such an understanding is beyond the immature spirit, and must be provided by a prompting from a deeper and more inward source.

But what of the actual candidate? In a ceremony, you may well say what you are prompted to say in order to get through the ceremony and be admitted to the group. But what is the real reason for putting up with it all? A real, honest attempt to answer this question about your desires and purposes as they actually are, rather than as you suppose they ought to be, is really the first step in initiation. It is one way of following the great maxim of the Delphic Oracle: *Gnothi seauton*, Know yourself.

One of the most common reasons for studying magic, though it may not be dominant in any particular person, is to gain magical powers. These are the same desires that, in other modes, provide markets for martial arts instruction, cosmetics and perfumes, the X-ray specs from comic book advertisements that supposedly let you see through people's clothes, courses in instant hypnotic power over others, and any number of other things. Some desire power as a means to other goals. Others simply wish to dominate others, often for the noblest and purest of reasons, since those they wish to dominate are clearly unable to do things correctly on their own. Similarly, there are those who crave power out of fear and a desire for protection from what they experience as a hostile and dangerous world.

Although this course does not explicitly set out to teach psychic "powers," the key to developing them is easy enough to describe. In fact, everyone reading this already knows it—whether they know they know it or not. The key to developing any skill is to use it, and to work at using it, with attention. We learn to walk by walking; we learn to run races by running races, noticing when we do well and when we do badly, and working to correct our running. We learn to read by reading, and to write by writing. There is no other way.

Coaching makes any of these things easier by far, of course, but the key is always to have a clearly formulated goal and to practice constantly with the goal in mind. Thus, to develop psychometric ability—the ability to get information from objects about their history and connections—the core practice is to touch objects with the intention of getting such information, note at each attempt the impressions (visual, auditory, emotional, or conceptual) that may arise, and test them against the facts as far as you can determine them.

Another set of reasons why people are attracted to occult and magical activities is the promise of knowledge. This may range from simple curiosity to a desire to know the real rather than conventional limits of what can be known to a hostile "prove it" skepticism that masks, perhaps, a desire to be convinced. Some people are attracted by the promise of pleasures of various kinds—by beauty, a desire to experience the unusual or outré, a delight in costumes, or the pleasure of association with others in a group of the secretly (or not so secretly) superior, or of the like-minded. Others are collectors and accumulators who wish to know in order to have more knowledge, more titles, or more exotic hats to add to their hoarded possessions.

There is at least one more class of motives, those having to do with a desire or thirst for meaning, for an inner coherence to existence that makes it more than simply a succession of moments following each other like random beads strung by a bored child. This desire often expresses itself in a derailed sort of way, as a habitual heaping-up of possessions, a search for more intense or exotic pleasures, a quest to increase your sphere of authority or influence, or a drive to know more and more (often about less and less). For those in whom it emerges on its own, however, the other kinds of motives often lose at least some of their charm.

A little later in this lesson, we will present an exercise that draws upon these considerations and helps you explore some of your own motivations in this work. Such exercises can have a tendency to veer off into either self-admiration or self-reproach, to sort out motives such as these into the simpler categories of "right" and "wrong," and to preen or punish the self accordingly.

A certain kind of writing in the Western esoteric tradition has tended to reinforce this habit by going on at great length about "right" and "wrong" motives for esoteric study, and to dismiss those who have "wrong" motives with scorn or lurid threats. While there is a certain justification for this sort of attitude—a good deal of damage has been done down through the years by people whose desires for, say, sexual exploitation or financial enrichment have been channeled into magic—it is still overly simplistic. Indeed, it can too easily provide an excuse for the sort of avoidance of self-knowledge we discussed before.

The transformation of motives is indeed a part of the work of magic, one aspect of that greater Work that is the transmutation of the whole self. The first step in that Work, however, must be a clear and nonjudgmental knowledge of what it is that is to be transmuted. Some of the exercises in this part of your studies lay groundwork for this knowledge. These include the exercises aimed at bringing about change in yourself, for the self (and its motives) are anything but static, and it is often under the stress of change that their authentic shape becomes most clearly visible.

HARΠOΠY AΠD SACRiFiCE: †iPHARE†H

Although Tiphareth is associated with harmony, many of its symbols and emblems are associated with death, and the *microprosopus*—the "lesser countenance" or aspect of divinity or the self—is traditionally more allied with severity than with mercy (which pertains to the *macroprosopus*, the "greater countenance" in Kether).

One reason for this link with severity is that the lesser countenance is a diminished and restricted form of the greater countenance. Another is that, despite the limitations of the microprosopus, the ordinary personality, the ordinary conscious self, must undergo a kind of decentering or recentering transformation before it can come to know the realm of Tiphareth. At its most basic level, this decentering occurs as the ordinary self begins to realize that it is not autonomous, that it is not the center and source of all its own activities and transformations, but that it is an element within a larger field—a field with which it is not identical, but which is, at the same time, not exactly alien to it or other than it.

One very important point to keep in mind is that, although this "higher self" is more than the physical or conscious aspects of a person, it is not separate from them. You don't need to reject your body or your ego to make contact with your higher self. In fact, your body and your ego, and your "outer world" as well, are all fields of action of your higher self. You don't so much make contact with your higher self as recognize the contact that already exists. But in recognizing this contact, you begin to lose your exclusive identification with your physical or social existence, and to see the ways in which these and other aspects of experience are expressions of an organizing center or principle that manifests through yourself and your experiences.

At the same time, the symbolism of sacrifice, crucifixion, death, and suspension is not simply a matter of jocular false faces put on to make things more impressive. Although this contact with your higher self can begin with a relatively simple shift of viewpoint or emphasis, it is not simply a matter of intuitive reorientation, and

even less a matter of exercising cleverness to solve some paradoxi-
cal puzzle. The alchemists said of their art that it requires everything you have, and the sacrifice of Tiphareth requires no less than
everything of us.

One less complete, but very important, mode of this transforming sacrifice is found in the experience of the kind of insupportable
dilemma that can dominate your experience. It often happens that, at
some point in your life, you find yourself caught in an intellectual,
moral, or spiritual antinomy, a dilemma constituted of two things
that cannot both be true, yet must both be true. This is a challenge
unto death.

Sometimes you can turn your back on it, embracing one of the
alternatives and refusing to recognize the other. But if you can stay
embedded in the dilemma despite its insolubility, a kind of reorientation takes place in the depths of the darkness, and a kind of solution arises—almost in spite of itself, or yourself. The emergence of this
solution is the work of what Jung calls the "transcendent function"
of the psyche. The Western esoteric tradition calls this source, among
other names, the higher self. It is one mode of action of Tiphareth
(although there is a higher mode of the same phenomenon that occurs
beyond Daath).

This kind of radical reorientation to the terms of a dilemma has two
results. Not only is the dilemma resolved, but consciousness is reori-
ented to some extent toward its own depth. You begin to awaken to
your foundations in the "higher" self. Avoiding the dilemma is an avoidance of this depth, and this is true culturally as well as individually.

The current situation of Western culture, as it has developed since
the late 17th century and especially in the last century, is an example
of this sort of cultural encounter with an insupportable dilemma.
There are many obvious examples of avoidance of the dilemma as

well, in retreats into the simplifications of fundamentalism or scientism, or the borrowing of the trappings of other more "spiritual" cultures, or the adoption of a disdainful and obscurantist "traditionalist" esotericism more focused on the supposed inaccuracies of others than on understanding and transforming the self.

These dilemmas are painful, wrenching, disruptive. If you can bear with them, however, they are profoundly transforming. The problem, as an alchemist might say, is to be sure that the vessel in which the reaction occurs is strong enough to contain the process from beginning to end.

SYMBOLISM OF TIPHARETH

As part of this lesson's work, you will learn a number of the symbols traditionally assigned to the sixth sephirah. These are as follows:

Divine name: *YHVH ALVH VDAaTh* (pronounced "Yeh-ho-wah Ell-o-ah Vah Dah-ath")

Archangel: Michael, "He who is as God"

Angelic order: Malakim, "Kings"

Astrological correspondence: Shemesh, the Sun

Tarot correspondence: the four sixes of the deck

As in previous lessons, commit these correspondences to memory and write the first four into the four circles of Tiphareth on your Tree of Life diagram. Then color the rest of Tiphareth golden yellow.

THE TWENTY-FOURTH, TWENTY-FIFTH, AND TWENTY-SIXTH PATHS

Learn the basic symbolism of the paths of the Tree descending from Tiphareth to other sephirah, then practice them with the aid of the corresponding tarot trumps. The paths and their symbolism are as follows:

Twenty-fourth path

> *Position on the Tree*: Tiphareth to Netzach
>
> *Hebrew letter*: נ, Nun
>
> *Tarot correspondence*: Trump XIII, Death
>
> *Astrological correspondence*: Scorpio

Twenty-fifth path

> *Position on the Tree*: Tiphareth to Yesod
>
> *Hebrew letter*: ס, Samech
>
> *Tarot correspondence*: Trump XIV, Temperance
>
> *Astrological correspondence*: Sagittarius

Twenty-sixth path

> *Position on the Tree*: Tiphareth to Hod
>
> *Hebrew letter*: ע, Ayin
>
> *Tarot correspondence*: Trump XV, the Devil
>
> *Astrological correspondence*: Capricorn

READING

Continue with the reading exercise as before, selecting sentences from your text and keeping company with them in the spare moments of your day. During the two weeks you spend on this lesson, pay attention to those events in each day that show a noticeable relation to the sentence for that day. Don't overdo this; the point of the exercise is not to jump on such events in the manner of a cat jumping on mice. Rather simply be aware and notice when a theme from your reading shows up in the events of your daily life. As always, keep notes in your magical journal.

WILL EXERCISE

One of the barriers you must sometimes overcome in the early stages of magical study is an aversion to admitting your own ignorance. The desire for knowledge, as mentioned above, is one of the major motives for magical study. As often as not, this desire is mingled with the desire to have other people think that you possess knowledge, and it is not far from there to a pose or simulacrum of knowledge that exists only in the admiring eyes, real or imagined, of others.

Yet the recognition of the limits of your knowledge is an essential step in any form of learning. As the well-known Zen parable puts it, it's impossible to pour tea into a teacup that is already full. Equally, the oracle at Delphi called Socrates the wisest of the Greeks because he alone knew that he knew nothing. The will exercise assigned for this lesson will alert you, in a small way, to the limits of your own knowledge and, in the process, continue developing the habits of awareness and action that lead to the perfection of the magical will.

For this exercise, identify a subject about which you know absolutely nothing. Any subject imaginable will do — the geography of Uzbekistan, the history of the Egyptian Middle Kingdom, the musical structure of jazz, the sexual habits of snails, the evidence for (or against) UFOs, or anything else, provided that you don't know a thing about it and that you have no reason to need or want to learn about it other than the performance of the exercise.

Once you've chosen your subject, decide to learn about it, and do so in detail and depth. Don't be satisfied with the sort of brief summary treatment found in encyclopedias or the shallower Internet-based research tools. Visit libraries, museums, and other resources; talk to people who have studied the subject; read books and, if you wish, watch videos and visit Web sites. How deeply you get into your research will depend, of course, on the amount of spare time you can put into it during the two weeks. For that two-week period, however, make it an obsession. Plan on visiting at least one place you've never been before in search of information on your subject.

When you finish this lesson, bring your studies to an end, at least for the time being. (If the subject turns out to be fascinating, you can always take it up again later.) As always, take notes on the experience in your magical journal.

SELF-TRANSMUTATION FOLLOW-UP

For the last two weeks, you have worked with a simple technique for reshaping aspects of yourself. Any number of things may have happened in that time. You may have noted improvements in the direction you desired; you may have noticed no change at all, or even a worsening in the situation; you may have become aware of something unexpected coming out of the exercise; you may have realized that the choice you made, or the perceptions behind it, were flawed or wholly inaccurate.

All of these outcomes are valuable, although their value may not be instantly apparent. (In fact, the first of them—simple success—may be the least useful in terms of the broader work of this course.) For now, discontinue the practice and, for the next two weeks, observe the aspect of yourself you sought to change. Note down in your journal anything that catches your attention.

MOTIVE EXPLORATION EXERCISE

This exercise follows up on the discussion of motives for esoteric study at the beginning of this lesson, which spoke of several different categories of reasons why you, or anyone, takes up the study of magic: desire for power, for knowledge, for pleasure, for sheer accumulation, and for meaning. You may be able to think of other categories, and trying to do so is part of your assignment here. But the core of the assignment is to examine the whole ensemble of your motives for taking up this study without indulging in self-reproach or self-admiration, and to distinguish the different classes into which these motives fall.

Some students find a written list useful in this work; nearly all find that time and a certain amount of brooding play an important part. Whatever route you find best, however, it should end with a list of categories, each of which has one or more specific motives under it.

Next, try to assign these classes of motive to the symbolic scheme of the five elements. (If you are familiar enough with another system—for example, the seven planetary powers, or twelve zodiacal signs—and find that your motives seem to fit these classifications better than they do the elemental scheme, feel free to use the other system instead.)

Your goal is to describe in one or two paragraphs the system of classes of motives you have developed in this way. Describe the classes of motives and how they correspond to the symbolic system (of elements, or of some alternative), and give examples of specific possible motives in each class. These examples do not have to be your own. Although you need not pass on to anyone else the details of any of the self-analyses you carry out, it is a real part of your training to learn to be aware of your own actual inner state. Carry out this elementary self-analysis, write it up, and store it in a secure place. As you progress along your path, there will come a point when it will be very helpful to review what you have done.

MEDITATION

Continue with the method of symbolic work introduced in lesson 4. For the next two weeks, the topic for your meditations is the four sixes of the tarot. As the expressions of Tiphareth, the central sphere of the Tree, through the four elements and Four Worlds, these cards symbolize some of the most important practical principles of the Western esoteric tradition. As before, work with one card in each session of meditation, and feel free to draw on this lesson's reading assignment and your other studies.

Here, as with your earlier meditative work with the tarot, come up with a single word that best expresses the meaning of each of the cards and commit these words to memory.

Plan on doing at least eight sessions of meditation during the next two weeks. As before, on every day you do not meditate, do the relaxation and attention exercise given in lesson 3.

Ritual

Perform the Middle Pillar exercise each day during the time you spend on this lesson. As you work with this rite over the next two weeks, concentrate on seeing it as far as possible as a unity, a single act, rather than as a collection of disparate gestures and sounds. Pay attention to any factors that seem to influence your ability to perceive this.

Lesson Review

1. Perform the meditation or attention exercise each day (see pages 152 and 51).
2. Perform the daily recollection each day on going to bed (see page 20).
3. Perform the Middle Pillar exercise each day (see page 107).
4. Perform the reading exercise every day (see page 31).
5. Work on the will exercise described above throughout the two weeks you spend on this lesson.
6. Work with the motive-exploration exercise described above, and the follow-up to last lesson's self-transmutation exercise.
7. Continue working on the number exercise presented in lesson 7.
8. Keep a record of your work.

When you have worked with these practices for at least two weeks, and accomplished at least the minimum of work given above, you are ready to go on to lesson 11.

LESSON 11

THE GREAT WORK

The purpose of these lessons, among other goals, has been to give you some exposure to the role of self-knowledge and self-perception in the Western esoteric tradition. The work of gaining a dispassionate understanding of the self is, in some sense, a lifelong task, but a certain approximation of it is one of the essentials of progress along the esoteric path.

There are a number of reasons, some of which we have already mentioned, why knowledge of the self is so important in this work. One reason in particular, however, cuts to the heart of the magician's way. The self and the universe, as we have explained, mirror each other in magical thought. To understand the self, then, is to understand the universe. To learn to reshape the self, similarly, is to gain, in some sense, the ability to reshape the universe. And to perfect the self—the goal of the magician's work, seen from the perspective of the microcosm, the "little universe" that is the self—leads, in an ultimate sense, to the perfection of the universe as well.

This is the alchemical Great Work in its widest and highest form, and the final goal of all the strange words and stranger deeds, the philosophies and obfuscations and reworked superstitions of the magical path. Being the final goal, it may seem preposterously far off to you at this basic phase of your training. Still, as the old alchemical axiom has it, the end is in the beginning. Some awareness of the purpose of this training may contribute to making sense of its odd and rather roundabout route.

One of the accusations routinely made against mystics, and not in modern Western cultures alone, is that those who take the path of inner transformation turn away from their responsibilities to the world around them—that they dive into their own navels and vanish, so to speak, leaving their environment and their fellow human beings no better off than before. This criticism has some merit, at least in some cases. Our present culture, moreover, is far from the first to seek mysticism and magic as a refuge from a failure to deal with life.

To some extent, however, this accusation is simply a matter of narrow perspective on the part of the accusers. Everyone, even mystics, has an effect on others and on the world. The most reclusive hermit lives somewhere and eats something, and the manner in which he lives and eats has its effect. This is one of the ways in which the transformation of the self helps bring about the transformation of the world. A great deal of human evil and destructiveness comes out of ignorance and simple folly, and a modest amount of self-knowledge and willed change can spare other people and other beings much in the way of suffering.

On the other hand, it is not uncommon for criticism of mystics as self-absorbed and selfish to come from those who advocate political or social agendas, and become incensed that practitioners of mystical paths are slow to adopt them. Certain trends in language and society have tended to make this sort of irritation a growing issue in modern times. The language of politics in our age has increasingly tended to mimic that of spirituality—"liberation," "vision," "God-given rights," and a whole range of overtly theological concepts have intruded into the political arena on both sides of the political spectrum, with consequent losses in the ability to compromise or even to think rationally about many issues.

Despite the similarities in terminology, however, the liberation sought by mysticism and magic and that sought by politics are two very different things. The most critical difference between them is that esoteric liberation must be sought freely by the individual. Self-knowledge and self-discipline cannot be legislated into being or enforced in the courts. Much less can the insight or wisdom sought and gained by these tools be imposed by any political means. What can be legislated and enforced by political methods is public belief and public obedience—things that have nothing to do with the esoteric path, and everything to do with political power.

The Hermetic tradition, in turn, has a long and murky history of involvement with schemes for political change, many of them seeking the imposition of some Utopian order on the world at large. These schemes have a special fascination for some people within the tradition, who see the chaos and suffering around them and are sure that a little well-meant guidance could spare people in general a good deal of pain. At the same time, the skills taught in esoteric circles can be used in the political arena with fair success; at least one modern scholar of magical traditions has pointed out that current advertising methods are all but indistinguishable from certain kinds of traditional symbolic magic.

Such projects, however, rarely succeed; politics demands skills beyond those practiced by magicians, a fact few magicians who go into politics seem to grasp. This is a good thing, for Utopias-made-concrete have an unpleasant habit of going sour—or septic. Imperfect beings and a "perfect" society make for a disastrous mix.

In this context, the tradition of withdrawal from political life practiced by many mystics and magicians makes a good deal of sense, and has been codified into a strict rule of political noninvolvement in some modern magical orders. You may find it useful to think about this rule, and to explore your own perceptions of the differences between political and esoteric ways of dealing with the ideas of transformation and freedom.

READING

Continue the reading exercise you performed in previous lessons. By this time, you have probably finished the first of your three texts, and you may already be well into the second. These books may differ sharply in prose style and opinion, but there may be other, subtler differences in the way the writers approach the complex task of communicating magical ways of looking at the world.

You may have noticed that the themes and ideas of your daily reading sometimes seem to exert a magnetism on the events of your daily life. Many students report that events relevant to a given sentence seem to show up with surprising frequency on the day when that sentence is the focus of the reading exercise. Others note resonances between sentences and dreams, or other expressions of the inner landscape of awareness. Both these experiences, and others like them, result from the power of intentionality—the orientation of awareness toward a particular way of approaching the universe that is the foundation of the magical will.

If you have not noticed anything of this sort, simply continue to practice the reading exercise, and attend to its other benefits—the reorientation of the mind from trivia to issues that matter, and the opportunity to study important magical texts in a focused manner. If you have noticed the effects of intentionality in the reading exercise, attend to them without trying to force them in one way or another. In either case, keep notes on your experience in your magical journal.

WİLL EXERCİSE

While the subtle training of intentionality has much to offer and leads to the heights of magical attainment, there is also much to be said for the simpler and less elevated work of learning habits of willed action. It is not necessary to launch fireworks from your fingertips to accomplish literally magical changes in your life. All that is required is the ability to act when action is appropriate, and to refrain from action when it is not.

The following exercise is designed to work on the second half of this statement. In order to practice it, you need a small, brightly colored object, a clock, and a room where you can spend some time undisturbed.

1. Put the bright object somewhere in the room where it can be seen easily. Put the clock in a different part of the room; you should be able to look at the clock without seeing the object.
2. Leave the room.
3. Wait a few minutes, and then go back into the room. Stay in it for at least five minutes.
4. During that time, do not look at the object, directly or indirectly. Keep your eyes turned away from it for the entire time.

Repeat the exercise at least four times during the two weeks you spend on this lesson. Keep notes on the experience in your magical journal.

TAROT: THE TRUMPS

This exercise can be done in a single sitting, or broken up into two sections, as you prefer. Allow about ninety minutes for the entire exercise, or about forty-five minutes for each of the two sections if done separately. Do each part of this exercise at least once, and you may find it useful to do it several times before you begin the next lesson.

1. Lay out the trumps in the pattern given in figure 11 (below).
2. Study each vertical pair, beginning with 0-XI. The image and title of each trump will mean something to you, whether you have any exposure to the esoteric traditions behind them or not. What do these paired images and names express to you as a pair? What do they express as two separate cards interacting? What light does each card in a pair cast on the other? What symbols do they have in common? What contrasts and oppositions do you find between them? Take notes on what you observe.

0	I	II	III	IV	V	VI	VII	VIII	IX	X
XI	XII	XIII	XIV	XV	XVI	XVII	XVIII	XIX	XX	XXI

Figure 11. Primary layout for the Tarot Trumps exercise.

3. Once you have considered the layout in figure 11, reverse the order of the second row of cards so that the numerical order runs right to left, as shown in figure 12. Repeat the study process in step 2, starting with 0-XXI. Take notes as before.
4. Compare the implications of the two different pairings for each of the trumps. This step doesn't need to take much time or

O	I	II	III	IV	V	VI	VII	VIII	IX	X
XXI	XX	XIX	XVIII	XVII	XVI	XV	XIV	XIII	XII	XI

Figure 12. Reverse layout for the Tarot Trumps exercise.

effort; simply compare the notes you've made. Make any additional notes that come to mind.

Now move on to the second part of the exercise, either as a continuation of the first, or in a separate sitting.

1. Lay out the trumps in a circle on the floor or a table, beginning with the Fool, reversed, about three to five card-lengths in front of you.
2. Place Justice upright directly in front of you.
3. Fill the space to either side with the other trumps in numerical order, continuing around the circle clockwise from the Fool to Justice and from Justice to the World, which is immediately to the left of the Fool, as shown in figure 13 (see page 162). Place each card facing outward from the center of the circle.
4. Get up and walk around the circle. Look at the flow of images from one card to another.
5. Walk around the circle again, but this time, as you pass each card, scan the circle to find the two cards with which each was paired in the first part of the exercise.
6. Look at the interactions between the cards, and where the cards are located in the circle. Write up your observations in your magical record.

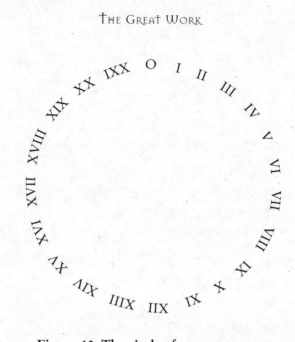

Figure 13. The circle of tarot trumps.

MEDITATION

This lesson's meditative work follows the approach introduced in lesson 7. Instead of working with the symbols of a sephirah in your meditations, however, explore the meanings and implications of a brief text. Keep the framework of the meditation—the sequence of opening, relaxation, rhythmic breathing, etc.—the same; just change the focus of consciousness. Use these three questions to focus your thought:

Where have I come from?

Where am I going?

What am I?

In your meditations, try to answer these as completely and accurately as possible. Take one of them at a time, and devote at least four sessions of meditation to each. In one or more sessions, you may find that no answer presents itself at all. If this happens, keep trying, and keep your thoughts focused on the question no matter how difficult, boring, or annoying this becomes.

As before, ten minutes of actual meditation in each session is sufficient. During the two weeks you spend on this lesson, do the attention exercise on any day in which you do not do a meditation.

THE MIDDLE PILLAR EXERCISE: FIRST EXPANSION

You have now been practicing the form of the Middle Pillar exercise presented in lesson 7 for close to two months. That form is the first and most basic phase of an exercise that can easily be developed. In this lesson, you will move on to the second phase of this exercise — a more focused and specialized development of the energy centers of your subtle body.

1. Perform the complete Lesser Banishing Ritual of the Pentagram (see page 51).
2. Standing in the center of the banished space facing east, formulate the Middle Pillar in the same manner as you have been doing, one sphere at a time, vibrating the appropriate divine name for each sphere, with these two changes:
   • Visualize the spheres in colored rather than pure white light. The sphere above the crown of your head remains white, but the one at your throat should be light gray, that at your solar plexus golden, that at your genitals violet, and that beneath your feet intense black with a slight greenish tinge.

- Increase the time spent holding the visualization of each sphere. Between the first inhalation, when the sphere is built up, and the vibration of the name, set some number of slow even breaths—perhaps four. Do this at each of the spheres while holding the image in your mind as clearly and forcefully as you can.

3. Once the entire Middle Pillar has been established and visualized as a unity, turn your attention to the point of light far above your head. Breathing in, visualize a beam of white light streaming down from that distant point into the highest of the spheres, and flowing down through each of the spheres in turn until it reaches the sphere beneath your feet, where it stops.

4. Breathing out, visualize the five spheres radiating this new flow of energy outward, into your physical body and into a roughly egg-shaped region extending a few feet out from your body in all directions. Repeat this whole process four times.

5. Direct your attention down below your feet, all the way down to a point at the center of the Earth. Breathing in, visualize a beam of rich green light streaming up from that point to the sphere beneath your feet, and flowing up through each of the spheres in turn until it reaches the sphere above your head, where it stops.

6. Breathing out, visualize the five spheres radiating this energy outward into your physical and etheric bodies as before. Repeat this whole process four times.

7. Turn your attention to the sphere you have formulated at your solar plexus. Breathing in, draw the air you breathe down to the solar plexus center, and visualize that center shining with an ever more intense golden light.

8. Breathing out, try to see and feel that light streaming outward in all directions, through your body and the egg-shaped area surrounding it. Repeat this whole process four times.
9. Perform the Qabalistic Cross once more to complete the exercise (see page 38).

This phase of the Middle Pillar exercise, like the last, should be performed daily, preferably at the same time each day. Please review the instructions in lesson 7, as well as these, to be sure of your grasp of the details.

LESSON REVIEW

1. Perform the meditation or attention exercise each day (see pages 162 and 51).
2. Perform the daily recollection each day on going to bed (see page 20).
3. Perform the Middle Pillar exercise as described above each day.
4. Perform the reading exercise as described above every day.
5. Perform the will exercise described above at least four times.
6. Perform both parts of the Tarot Trumps exercise given above.
7. Continue working with the number exercise given in lesson 7.
8. Keep a record of your work.

When you have worked with these exercises for at least two weeks, and have completed at least the minimum requirements given above, you are ready to proceed to lesson 12.

LESSON 12

THE VEIL OF THE SANCTUARY

This course has taken you on a passage down the Tree of Life—not merely in terms of the symbols and teachings covered, but in certain elements of underlying structure as well. Ideas that emerged in the first lesson that were stated in their simplest form in the second have returned as more and more complex concepts and practices in the following lessons.

With this lesson, both the symbolic and structural passages down the Tree come within the realm of ordinary experience. The sephiroth you study in this lesson and the three following—Netzach, Hod, Yesod, and Malkuth, the quaternary that forms the lowest section of the Tree of Life—form the world of everyday life. Their equivalents in the microcosm of human consciousness—the emotions, the intellect, the range of subtle perceptions often called "intuition," and the five physical senses—provide most of the tools with which human beings make their way through that world.

This may not be immediately obvious. It may be less obvious still why the human functions that correspond to the higher sephiroth do not play an equal role.

A careful examination of what actually goes on in your awareness, however, will reveal an interesting point. The higher functions, whether those of the upper levels of the ruach (memory, will, imagination) or those of the neshamah, chiah, or yechidah, usually appear (when they appear at all) in the guise of one of the four lower functions. Memory may take the form of a sensory image, will of an emotional drive, creative imagination of an idea or an intuitive sense of "rightness." Any of the higher aspects may take the form of any of the lower, but they rarely if ever appear in their own guise.

That the higher functions have their own forms distinct from the appearances mentioned here is a matter not only of magical theory, but of personal experience for many people. The memory that reaches out beyond a single image or idea to grasp the essence of some past time, the burst of will that overrides all inner and outer obstacles, the imagination that draws together myriad fragments of experience in an instant to make a single meaningful unity, these are things that happen on occasion to many human beings.

It is this occasional occurrence, of course, that is the sticking point. These experiences are uncommon and rarely repeatable at will. They represent occasional flickers of a level of functioning that, most of the time, is out of reach. It's worth noting, as well, that their equivalents in the lower functions (ordinary memory, will, and creative imagination) are notoriously unreliable.

You can think of this feature of human experience as a barrier, definite but permeable, separating the four lower from the six higher sephiroth. In the Qabalah, this barrier is called the Veil of the Sanctuary. There is a great deal of theoretical material in Qabalistic writings about the origins, nature, and purpose of this veil, but at this point these are less significant than the fact of the veil itself— and the possibility of its opening.

For the veil can be parted, deliberately, in a transformation of awareness carried out by way of the technical processes of meditation and magic. This is one way of describing the primary work of the magician in the Western esoteric tradition.

The parting of the veil has as its first object the attainment of the phase of consciousness symbolized by Tiphareth, not only the closest of the higher sephiroth to the veil, but the natural center of the ruach, the conscious self, as well. In this sense, the opening of the Veil of the Sanctuary can also be seen as an act of recentering in which consciousness enters into a place of balance and the rest of the self comes into proper alignment around it.

This recentering is a radical transformation, with radical effects. It does not, on the other hand, bring about perfection. Nor is it the end of the process of transmutation. Quite the contrary: the purpose of this primary work is to open up possibilities, not close them off for good.

EMOTION: NETZACH

Netzach is the sphere of myriad energies experienced in ordinary consciousness as moods and emotional states. One of the features of moods, and of the energies of Netzach generally, is that they manifest not so much in the form of objects of awareness as in that of alterations of awareness. When you are angry, you don't see anger, you see the object or target of your anger through the anger and colored by it. The same is true of other moods and emotions. In fact, all the sephiroth on the side of mercy have to do more with the qualities of consciousness than its objects.

Since the energies of the sphere of Netzach manifest as alterations in the act of knowing or perceiving rather than in the object of perception, it is generally much easier to identify with them—that is, to take your own feelings too personally. Feeling anger, it is easy to conclude that you are angry. The problem with this conclusion is that it can go beyond a mere descriptive statement. It can become a policy statement, or a basic plank in the platform of your sense of who you are. This, in turn, means that you come to see moods as "all in your head," a function of your own nature, thus devaluing them. From an esoteric point of view, moods are the manifestation of energies, and can transcend the merely personal in the same way that the abstract structures of mathematics transcend the minds that perceive them.

What Yeats called "the fire-born moods" are manifestations in us of impersonal energies that are in play all around us and throughout our world. A significant part of magical training has to do with learning to sense these energies and recognize their autonomous functioning in the world. Yet another has to do with intentional control of these energies by evocation and invocation. To invoke the moods of the cosmos without being swept away by them, however, you must first experience the moods of ordinary life without being dominated by them. Thus another aspect of magical work involves strengthening your ability to work with energies by working with moods and establishing channels through which they can flow without risk of damage.

The four functions of awareness mapped out in Jungian psychology (feeling, intellect, intuition, and sensation) can be aligned with the four traditional elements and the humors. In fact, you can learn a great deal from considering the correspondences between these different schemes. A very important point that is often insufficiently appreciated is that there are two ways in which each of these functions of the psyche can manifest: superior (integrated) or inferior (unintegrated).

A person who is subject to strong, dominating moods is not necessarily a "feeling" type; instead, such a person may have a poorly integrated feeling function. Similarly, a person whose thoughts are dominated by some set of ideas may well have a poorly integrated intellectual function. An integrated function is available for use and is under conscious control. An unintegrated, undeveloped function acts autonomously and intrusively.

In magical work, you must be sure that your own energies are integrated and in equilibrium if you want to invoke the energies of the world. Failure to do so may lead to disruption or domination by uncontrollable moods.

SYMBOLISM OF NETZACH

As part of this lesson's work, you will learn a selection of the symbols traditionally assigned to the seventh sephirah. These are as follows:

Divine name: YHVH TzBAVTh (pronounced "Ye-ho-wah Tza-ba-oth")

Archangel: Haniel, "Grace of God"

Angelic order: Tarshishim, "Shining Ones"

Astrological correspondence: Nogah, the planet Venus

Tarot correspondence: the four sevens of the deck

As before, commit these correspondences to memory and write the first four into the four circles of Netzach on your Tree of Life diagram. Then color the rest of Netzach green.

THE TWENTY-SEVENTH, TWENTY-EIGHTH, AND TWENTY-NINTH PATHS

Learn the basic symbolism of the paths descending the Tree from Netzach, then test and rehearse your knowledge using the corresponding tarot trumps. The paths and symbols of these paths are as follows:

Twenty-seventh path

> *Position on the Tree*: Netzach to Hod
>
> *Hebrew letter*: פ, Peh
>
> *Tarot correspondence*: Trump XVI, the Tower
>
> *Astrological correspondence*: Mars

Twenty-eighth path

> *Position on the Tree*: Netzach to Yesod
>
> *Hebrew letter*: צ, Tzaddi
>
> *Tarot correspondence*: Trump XVII, the Star
>
> *Astrological correspondence*: Aquarius

Twenty-ninth path

> *Position on the Tree*: Netzach to Malkuth
>
> *Hebrew letter*: ק, Qoph
>
> *Tarot correspondence*: Trump XVIII, the Moon
>
> *Astrological correspondence*: Pisces

READING

Continue the reading exercise as in previous, lessons. Pay attention to the way this exercise relates to your emotional life during the two weeks you spend on this lesson. It may also be worthwhile to note the role of mood and emotional state in your choice of sentences.

WILL EXERCISE

The realm of Netzach, of mood and emotion, has important points of contact with the realm of will. In Qabalistic terms, Netzach carries the reflection of Geburah, the sephirah of will, below the Veil of the Sanctuary. To say the same things in the language of ordinary experience, emotional states often serve as a substitute for will in those who have not yet developed the higher powers of their ruach. Those who can't carry out a difficult but necessary action on the basis of pure will can often work themselves up to it in a rush of strong emotion.

On this fact rests much of the propaganda of wartime and the image of the passionately emotional hero. On a less noble level, the advertising industry makes its money by evoking in consumers emotional states that convert readily into the act of purchasing a product. As these examples may suggest, however, the person who requires emotional incentives to act is limited, and can be controlled with relative ease.

One of the necessary stages in magical training is learning to distinguish between emotion and will. This has sometimes been misinterpreted as a rejection of the emotional realm of experience, but it is an axiom of magic that no part of the self can be discarded in this way. Rather, the work that needs to be done is simply a process of recognizing that emotion and will are not the same thing, and developing the ability to act on the basis of will and not simply that of emotion.

The following exercise helps you explore this aspect of magical training.

1. Choose an activity that you actively dislike and do it as often as possible during the first week you spend on this lesson.
2. Pay attention to the way your thoughts and emotions react to the experience.
3. In the second week, choose an activity you enjoy, and again, do it as often as possible, paying attention to your reactions.
4. Compare the two sets of experiences.

More generally, as you continue with your training, notice how often and in what ways your decisions and actions are shaped by your moods and feelings. When are these influences helpful? When are they not?

SELF-PERCEPTION EXERCISE: EMOTIONS

You've learned that the four lowest sephiroth on the Tree of Life are associated with four common functions of ordinary human awareness: Netzach with the emotions, Hod with the intellect, Yesod with the ill-defined set of perceptions usually lumped together as "intuition," and Malkuth with the ordinary physical senses. Under normal conditions, these four functions make up most of what goes on in the human mind. The exercises of the Western esoteric tradition do not count as "normal conditions," of course, and one of the results of working with these exercises is the emergence of other functions within your awareness. Nonetheless, these four common functions remain, and need to be explored and understood.

The following exercise helps you carry out some part of this work of exploration. In a certain sense, it is a follow-up to the self-perception exercise introduced in lesson 8. It involves, however, a more specific focus and a different approach.

1. For the next two weeks, be as aware of your emotional state and its transformations as you can. Try to do this, not for specified periods, but generally, throughout your ordinary activities.

2. When you do your daily recollection at the end of each day (see page 20), recall not only what you did, but how you felt, what your mood was.

3. As you go about your daily affairs, pay attention to your emotional reactions to events, as well as to feelings that may not seem to have any connection to what happens.

In this exercise, what you need is not the intense focus of, for instance, meditation, but rather a background awareness that will not interfere with your ordinary activities. This kind of background awareness is itself a magical technique of some importance, and worth developing. Some students find it comes easily; others have more trouble acquiring the knack. The reading exercise, has this same knack as one of its goals. Work on it in this additional way for the next two weeks, and keep notes on the results in your magical journal.

TAROT: STORYTELLING

For many people, the tarot deck is, first and foremost, a method of divination—that is, a means of obtaining information not otherwise available to consciousness, whether that information be about "the future" (a concept that itself begs a great many questions) or about hidden aspects of a present situation. While the tarot has many more uses in the Western esoteric tradition, its divinatory function is an important one. It can be a valuable tool for the magician in training.

Divination, however, is a more complex art than it may seem at first glance. When you divine with the tarot, you don't simply deal out a handful of cards and look up predetermined meanings. This sort of unintelligent approach to divination has led, in fact, to the diviner's art being little respected in our society at present.

A more useful (and accurate) way to approach the matter is to treat divination as a subset of the broader human art of storytelling. People have always told each other stories as a means of making sense of the world. The oldest mythic tales are also the deepest, in terms of their power to give shape and meaning to human experience. When you read a spread of tarot cards, you tell a story, taking some cards as characters, others as events, and still others as underlying forces that drive the story onward to its end.

The following exercise gives you some experience of this process and serves as a stepping-stone to the practice of tarot divination introduced later. Do the exercise at least four times during the two weeks you spend on this lesson; allow at least half an hour for each session.

1. Sit at (or on) a convenient flat surface, such as a table, a bed, or the floor, with your tarot deck within reach.
2. Begin with the usual opening gesture (see page 15), and then take out the deck and shuffle it at least three times.
3. Deal out between three and ten cards from the top of the deck, one at a time, turning them over as you set them down before you side by side in a line.
4. Consider the cards before you. Think of them as a sequence of images running from left to right, as though they were writing

in a picture alphabet. Or see them as panels in a comic strip from which the words are somehow left out.

5. If there are court cards present, try thinking of them as people involved in this collection of images: treat trumps with human figures as characters, and those with other images (the Tower, for instance) as situations or settings. If number cards appear, use your keywords or the images on the cards as seems best to you.

6. Make up a story out of the images before you. This does not have to be long or very detailed. A spread of three or four cards isn't likely to give material for more than a single incident. But the story should include all the cards in one way or another, and follow the progression of the cards from left to right. A few sentences' worth is enough for the purpose of this exercise. Write these sentences down, and close with the usual gesture.

This process may seem like child's play and, in an important sense, it is. Most children, unlike most adults, retain a quality of unself-conscious imagination that is one of the most useful elements of the diviner's art. If you approach this exercise in a playful manner, it is likely to prove more rewarding than if you attempt it in grim seriousness.

MEDITATION

Continue with the system of meditation on symbols first introduced in lesson 4. For the next two weeks, the topic for your meditation is the four sevens of the tarot deck. As before, come up with a single word describing the meaning of each card as you understand it, then commit these words to memory.

Do this meditation each day during the two weeks you spend on this lesson. As always, enter a full description of your meditations in your magical journal.

RITUAL

Perform the expanded Middle Pillar exercise given in lesson 11 each day during the two weeks you spend on this lesson. During these workings, pay particular attention to any emotional effects you may notice from the ritual. Does it have any effect on your mood? If so, is the effect consistent, or does it seem to vary from day to day? Keep notes on this in your magical journal.

LESSON REVIEW

1. Perform the meditation as described above each day.
2. Perform the expanded Middle Pillar exercise as described above each day.
3. Perform the daily recollection each day upon going to bed (see page 20).
4. Continue the reading exercise as described above.
5. Perform the will exercise described above during the next two weeks.
6. Perform the self-perception exercise described above over the next two weeks.
7. Do the Tarot Storytelling exercise described above four times during the time you spend on this lesson.
8. Continue working with the number exercise given in lesson 7.
9. Keep a record of your work.

When you have carried out these practices for at least two weeks, and have completed at least the minimum work required above, you are ready to proceed to lesson 13.

THE KEY OF CONSCIOUSNESS

One aspect of the Western esoteric tradition that has come in for a great deal of criticism in recent years is its allegedly negative attitude toward the physical, material universe. This same critique, for that matter, has been directed against traditional Western spirituality of all sorts. To critics of this stripe, spiritual teachings that allot any more value to the nonphysical than to the world of matter are "negative" and "world-hating," if not simply neurotic attempts to flee from the real world into a desert of arid intellectualism.

A certain amount of this criticism is simple partisan propaganda. Followers of several religious and philosophical viewpoints in the Western world—scientific materialism, certain neo-Pagan revivals, and several branches of liberal Christianity, among others—have found that the charge of "world-hating" makes a useful cudgel with which to belabor their doctrinal opponents.

Some of the criticism, by contrast, is probably merited. It's hard to argue against the claim that groups that, for example, practice castration as a means to ritual purity, or who hold that the physical universe is the creation of the devil and that humanity's one hope is to die out and get free of its worldly prison, are going overboard. On the other hand, such groups make up only a small part of the West's spiritual heritage, and even a smaller proportion of its esoteric traditions.

Perhaps the largest part of this common criticism, however, is based on simple misunderstanding. It is true, certainly, that in the Western esoteric tradition one ancient description of the goal of the work is the departure or disentangling of the soul from the realm of matter. It is, however, quite untrue that this implies contempt for the material world, and equally untrue that the removal of the soul is equivalent to the removal of the entire self.

The key to the whole matter is the idea that the human self exists on all levels of being. Each phase or aspect of the self, from yechidah to guph, has its proper equivalent along the spectrum of existence.

The problem arises because, as presently constituted, most human beings are partly out of phase with the universe around them. The ruach, the collection of powers you think of as your "ordinary personality," exists on the level of concrete consciousness, while its highest capacities deal with some levels of abstract consciousness. In most people, however, these are not the levels on which it functions. Instead, most of the time, it functions, more or less awkwardly, as if it existed on the plane of physical matter.

What does this mean in concrete terms? The ruach has the function of perception; it encounters things by perceiving them. However, it can only perceive things of its own level.

Take a moment, now, to look around the room in which you're sitting. Are you perceiving the room itself, the furniture, the paint on the walls? No. You are perceiving a mental image of the room, reflected onto the level of concrete consciousness. That image comes to you by way of a Rube Goldberg apparatus made up of bouncing photons, eye pigments, electrochemical nerve reactions, and complicated processes in the brain and mind. This, as any physicist can tell you, has next to nothing in common with the actual structure of matter, space, and time that surrounds you.

It's certainly true that this mental image is a good enough fit to allow you to get through everyday life. Problems arise, however, as soon as the mental image is confused with the material reality behind it. Even on a physical level, what is true from one perspective may not be true from another. Worse, the ruach becomes so used to the apparent solidities of its surroundings that it begins to treat things of its own level (memories, perceptions, beliefs) as though they were as solid as bricks, and to relate astral and physical perceptions in a whole series of confused and irrational ways.

It's worth noting, as well, that the entanglement of the ruach with the physical plane is not itself a conscious matter. It happens automatically, as the background to the ruach's conscious thought and feeling.

The problem, then, is not with the material world, but with the current structure of human consciousness. Nor is it necessary to flee from the world of matter, only to reorient your conscious mind so that it experiences its perceptions as perceptions rather than as solid things.

This process is the same one discussed in the last lesson as the parting of the Veil of the Sanctuary, seen from a slightly different perspective. A glance at the Tree of Life shows the connection. The sephiroth that are below the veil and symbolize the aspects of ordinary human consciousness are precisely those that link up directly to Malkuth, the sephirah of material existence. Those that do not have a direct link to Malkuth remain hidden, or at best function through one or more of those that do.

And this, again, is the situation the Western esoteric tradition seeks to transcend.

Intellect: Hod

Hod is the sphere of myriad structures and their endless manipulations. It is the proper sphere, not only of divinations based on models of the cosmos, but also of magical methods that involve the manipulation of components to form significant patterns.

This, in turn, leads to one of the great difficulties associated with Hod: that significance becomes identified with the patterns, and the attention of the practitioner becomes fixed on the patterns and structures themselves, haunted by the sense that somewhere there is a key manipulation that will produce the ultimate, self-explanatory pattern.

This is an error reminiscent of all those jokes about the guru who, when asked to reveal the meaning of life, answers "forty-two" or "a carrot." The problem lies in supposing that discovering the meaning of life is like solving the clues of a crossword puzzle. Life is not made meaningful by treating it as an object for consciousness. It is made meaningful through participation in it by consciousness. Structures become meaningful, not when we decode them, but when we live through them and thus make of them channels of life. The idea that sufficient cleverness of the puzzle-solving variety can solve "occult secrets" is an illusion. Esotericism is not a matter of hidden messages, but of depth upon depth of meaning, bringing to life the dead bones of the structures that embody it.

These structures have a twofold function. One, deriving in a sense from Chesed, is to serve as vehicles for meaning. The other, deriving in a sense from Geburah, is to limit and restrain the temptation to unfocused indulgence in either superficial cleverness or unbalanced energies.

Unbalanced energies often manifest as parts of the self, as urges or desires that resonate so closely with small imbalances in your own makeup that you take them for your own. It's possible to be swept away on a current of rage or desire, for example, identifying with it and never realizing that it is some impersonal energy that has manifested through the personality.

This is one of the functions of rules and regulations: to provide a system of coordinates against which breaches in balance can be detected. This is a standard theme in folk tales, in which success in a quest or some other activity depends on adherence to arbitrary rules. The rules may seem to have no connection with the quest until they are broken and the quest fails, or has only partial success.

The older psychoanalysts developed a classification of ways in which people deal with problems. Careful reflection on this classification can be very helpful for students of magic.

1. *Acting out:* People act on their contradictory desires and find themselves involved in recurrent self-defeating patterns or situations.
2. *Suffering out:* Some people, rather than acting without awareness, are aware of their impulses and desires but block their expression, experiencing instead a disruption of their inner lives.
3. *Working out:* Here, not only do conflicts affect consciousness, they are actually consciously recognized and examined, and (ideally, at any rate) resolved.

Embedded in this scheme is a model of increasingly conscious approaches to handling inner conflicts. The key is inhibition based on recognition. Realizing that some unconscious pattern is causing trouble, you refuse to act on impulses connected with it, thus forcing the conflict into conscious expression, first perhaps as an emotional turbulence, and then, with gradual attention, emerging into full consciousness as a pattern of desires, fears, and avoidances that needs to be resolved. Moreover, it can be resolved, once you recognize it for what it is.

This approach is especially useful in dealing with unbalanced impersonal energies when they manifest through your own consciousness. It is important to remember, as well, that it is precisely through consciousness (and the unconscious underpinnings of consciousness) that you encounter the inner world. Consciousness, in other words, is deepened by difficulties, which is why effective initiations always involve challenges.

SYMBOLISM OF HOD

As part of this lesson's work, you will learn a selection of the symbols traditionally assigned to the eighth sephirah. These are as follows:

Divine name: ALHIM TzBAVTh (pronounced "Ell-oh-heem Tza-ba-oth")

Archangel: Raphael, "Healing of God"

Angelic order: Beni Elohim, "Sons of Elohim"

Astrological correspondence: Kokab, the planet Mercury

Tarot correspondence: the four eights of the deck

As before, commit these correspondences to memory and write the first four into the four circles of Hod on your Tree of Life diagram. Then color the rest of Hod orange.

The Thirtieth and Thirty-first Paths

You will also learn the basic symbolism of the paths of the Tree that descend from Hod and practice and rehearse that knowledge with the aid of the corresponding tarot trumps. These paths and their symbolism are as follows:

Thirtieth path

Position on the Tree: Hod to Yesod

Hebrew letter: ר, Resh

Tarot correspondence: Trump XIX, the Sun

Astrological correspondence: Sun

Thirty-first path

Position on the Tree: Hod to Malkuth

Hebrew letter: ש, Shin

Tarot correspondence: Trump XX, Judgment

Astrological correspondence: the element of Fire

By now, you have learned and committed to memory the basic symbolism of nearly all the paths on the Tree. Now is a good time to go back over the symbolism studied and learned in previous lessons to make sure that you have mastered this first essential step in learning the symbolic alphabet of magic.

READING

Continue the reading exercise, reading one chapter from your text each week, selecting seven sentences from each and keeping company with one of those sentences each day. Over the next two weeks, pay particular attention to ways in which the reading exercise shapes your thoughts and the activity of your mind.

WILL EXERCISE

The activities of the thinking mind, like all other acts of the whole human being, need to be brought under the control of conscious will at times. On the most practical and commonsense level, there are situations in which you will find it necessary or useful to think clearly and intently about a particular topic, without the interference of irrelevant thoughts. On a deeper level, the ability to direct, focus, and silence your thinking mind at will forms a crucial part of your magician's inner toolkit.

A bit of folklore from Ireland is relevant here. Supposedly, when you encounter a leprechaun, you gain access to its pot of gold by the simple expedient of watching the creature steadily, without looking away from it for so much as a second. As long as your glance remains fixed on the leprechaun, it cannot escape and will eventually have to hand over its gold. Legends and folktales recount the ingenious tricks used by leprechauns in such circumstances to distract their would-be captors for an instant and make their escape.

This Irish story has become a fixture among teachers of meditation, because it provides a very adequate metaphor for the behavior and misbehavior of human consciousness. As with the leprechaun, the human mind can be forced to yield up treasures if it is confronted with unwavering attention. As with the leprechaun, however, the mind can be remarkably agile in finding ways to evade the observing gaze.

Your practice of meditation in earlier lessons has probably given you some taste of these evasions. In order to counter these, some systems of Hermetic magic include concentration exercises to develop the capacity for willed direction of attention and thought. The following exercise is one of the standard practices of this type, and has the added advantage of providing for a fairly good measure of your capacity for concentration and focus.

For this exercise, you need a clock or watch with a sweep second hand. Seated comfortably, place the clock or watch so that you can follow the movement of the second hand easily. Your task is to keep your gaze fixed on the point of the second hand for five full minutes. During this time, admit no other thoughts to your mind.

Most students are lucky to manage fifteen seconds of uninterrupted concentration at first. Keep trying for a total of five minutes. Do this exercise once a day for the two weeks you spend on this lesson. Keep track of the longest period of unbroken concentration you manage.

SELF-PERCEPTION EXERCISE: INTELLECT

The self-perception exercise introduced in lesson 12 had two principal purposes: to encourage you to be more aware of your usual moods and emotional fluctuations and to teach you a particular way of directing your awareness (a kind of "background noticing" that continues through the ordinary activities of life). Both purposes are part of a broader intention to show some of the uses of introspection and self-knowledge in the Western esoteric tradition.

In this lesson, we aim the same exercise at a different target: the intellect, the reasoning and symbolic mind in which information is processed and thinking takes place.

For many people, particularly in today's culture, this is a much harder target to hit than the emotions because of its sheer speed: in any five-minute period, you may experience five dozen thoughts on as many different subjects. If you tried to write down all the thoughts you had in one day, it would take you rather more than a day to do it! For the sake of sanity, as well as for other reasons, the background awareness you are striving to develop has a slightly different aim. Instead of trying to keep track of the subjects of your thought, notice its qualities—its quickness or slowness, its general tone (critical, enthusiastic, bored, wandering), and its exactness or vagueness. Does it repeat itself, or wander from subject to subject? Does it tend to take any one tone habitually? Be aware of these things, and of how they change over time.

As with lesson 12's self-perception exercise, work at developing this background awareness of thinking for the next two weeks, trying to keep it going throughout your waking hours. Keep track of your level of success in your magical record.

TAROT: PATTERNMAKING

The Tarot Storytelling exercise introduced one of the skills useful in the process of tarot divination. The free-flowing process of imaginative play with symbols is crucial to opening up the higher or deeper phases of your awareness—beyond the veil, where the information that comes through the tarot has its home ground.

This, however, is the "force" aspect of the diviner's art, as opposed to its "form" aspect. The same deep phases of the mind with which you seek to cooperate speak naturally in symbolic language, and that language is by no means random or disorganized. Rather, it tends to shape itself around patterns of ordered symbolism that are presented to the deeper mind by the surface of your awareness.

It is a commonplace of psychotherapy that patients of Freudian analysts tend to end up having Freudian dreams, while patients of Jungian analysts tend to have Jungian dreams. In the same way, students of the Western esoteric tradition find the symbols they have studied emerging from their own minds, in dreams, reverie, and divination. Some magicians in the past have taken this as proof of the objective truth of one or another system of symbolism, but what is actually happening is a function of a process we've discussed already: the aspects of the ruach above the veil make use of those below it to communicate.

The process of divination, then, combines a sensitivity to the play of symbols with an alertness to the way those symbols relate to each other and to the symbolic matrix of the diviner's own system of magic. The following exercise helps you learn the second of these elements, and continues your development toward tarot divination. Like the exercise in the last lesson, it should be done at least four times during the two weeks you spend on this lesson. Half an hour per session is a good amount of time to allow.

1. Sit at or on a convenient flat surface, such as a table, a bed, or the floor, with your tarot deck within reach. As before, begin with the opening gesture (see page 15), and then shuffle the deck at least three times.

2. Deal out between three and ten cards from the deck, one at a time, turning them face up as you set them side by side in a line before you.

3. Consider the cards before you. Instead of seeing them as images in a story, however, pay strict attention to their roles as elemental and magical symbols. Think of them as a progression of elements, running from left to right, each emerging and then

giving way to the one that follows it. Give the four suits their usual elemental meanings, and see the court cards as combinations of the elements. For the sake of this exercise, the trumps can be assigned to the element of spirit.

4. Pay special attention to the relationships between the elements. Traditional lore describes fire and water, and earth and air, as opposites. When cards of these elements are adjacent, the result is conflict. Adjacent cards of the same element tend to reinforce each other, while cards of elements that are not in opposition (earth and water, for instance) relate to each other harmoniously. The trumps, representing spirit, can be seen as harmonizing with all elements. The sequence of cards before you is thus a pattern of stresses and resolutions, with each card reacting to its neighbors as the whole moves from an initial situation to a conclusion.

5. Keep watch for two special situations in the cards. One is called the Pattern of Balance. This occurs when two cards in opposition are preceded or followed by a third card that harmonizes with both. An example is the Three of Wands and the Eight of Cups, with the Four of Pentacles either just before or just after them. When this occurs, the harmonizing card resolves the conflict between the two opposed cards, and the whole pattern is held to be harmonious. The other situation occurs when court cards interact with other elements. The minor elements in the court cards (for example, the fire in the King of Cups) also interacts with the elements of the other cards, influencing the relationship. Thus the King of Cups next to a Wand card creates less conflict than, for instance, the Queen of Cups in the same position. But the Queen of Wands strengthens other Wand cards less than the King does.

6. When you have a clear sense of the relationships between the cards, write down a brief description in your magical journal, and close with the usual gesture.

With practice, an awareness of the cards' interactions will come to you automatically as you consider a reading. The ability to do this is an important element of competence in tarot divination, and allows you to grasp the full implications of any given reading.

MEDITATION

Continue with the system of meditation on symbols introduced in lesson 4. For the next two weeks, the topic for your meditation is the four eights of the tarot deck. As before, come up with a single word describing the meaning of each card as you understand it, then commit these words to memory.

Do this meditation each day during the two weeks you spend on this lesson. As always, enter a full description of your meditations in your magical record.

RITUAL

Perform the expanded Middle Pillar exercise given in lesson 11 each day during the two weeks you spend on this lesson. During these workings, seek maximum clarity and precision in the visualizations and physical movements alike. Pay attention to the effects this may have on your experience of the exercise.

LESSON REVIEW

1. Perform the meditation as described above every day.
2. Perform the expanded Middle Pillar exercise as described above every day.
3. Perform the daily recollection every day upon going to bed (see page 20).
4. Continue to perform the reading exercise as described above.
5. Perform the will exercise described above each day for five minutes.
6. Perform the self-perception exercise described above during the two weeks you spend on this lesson.
7. Do the Tarot Patterning exercise described above at least four times.
8. Continue to work on the number exercise given in lesson 7.
9. Keep a record of your work.

When you have carried out these practices for at least two weeks, and have completed at least the minimum work listed above, you are ready to proceed to lesson 14.

LESSON 14

THE MEANS
OF MAGIC

In the last two lessons, we explored certain traditional perspectives on the principal work that confronts the magician—the parting of the Veil of the Sanctuary, the reorientation of consciousness to allow full access to the potentials of human awareness.

To have a goal is one thing; to have a functional method of achieving it can be another thing entirely. Traditional Western magic does offer a method, of course. Still, what are you to make of such a method? The pentacles and sigils, the names of God and words of power, the spirits and specters and visionary experiences of the magical tradition may resemble many things —advanced psychosis among them, some may say—but they have very little visibly in common with the considerations we have been discussing. Does the reintegration of the self really require knowledge of the names of archangels?

In one entirely valid sense, of course, the answer is no. It is wholly possible to pass through the Veil of the Sanctuary without the baroque apparatus of ceremonial magic and Qabalistic meditation. Other spiritual traditions, powerful and effective ones, use far simpler methods to achieve a comparable end.

From another perspective, however, this is the same as saying that it's possible to build a house with nothing but an axe. This is unquestionably true, but at the same time, there are some fairly sharp limitations on the kind of house you can build with an axe, and the addition of a few other tools can both expand the range of available possibilities and simplify a great deal of the work. Add an entire carpenter's toolkit and both the possibilities and the process benefit even more, even though some of the tools in that toolkit seem, in their own way, remarkably strange.

The toolkit of the Western esoteric tradition contains a great many tools, ranging from simple to complex, from straightforward to bizarre, and from broadly effective to extremely specialized or even largely useless. With every generation, new tools have been added, old ones modified or reconditioned, and a few thrown out, although even these tend to get tossed back in later on. Just as the tools in a carpenter's kit all derive their effectiveness from a few simple principles of physics, the tools in the magician's kit all make use of a small number of factors.

Most important of these are the three aspects of human consciousness we discussed at some length earlier—imagination, will, and memory. Each of the exercises of Western esotericism draws on at least one of these, and most rely on all three: imagination builds the forms; will energizes them; memory provides the context and incorporates the effect of the practice into the structure of future acts of awareness.

These three aspects of the self also share a common place in the traditional symbolism of human consciousness: all are parts of the ruach that lie above the Veil of the Sanctuary, and all normally function only indirectly, through one of the lower aspects of the self.

This indirect and often unsteady functioning, however, points to a critical issue. Any human potential that has not been exercised or developed—a muscular movement, a kind of thinking, an artistic talent, or anything else—tends to show itself in this way. In a sense, then, the Veil of the Sanctuary is simply the line between those faculties most of us have developed and those most of us have neglected. In this same sense, the practices of magic are the calisthenics or "five-finger exercises" of imagination, will, and memory, meant to develop these to their full potential strength.

Such an interpretation of magic may seem to offer little room for the powers and odd abilities normally associated with magical traditions. This is true, however, only if the possibilities of memory, imagination, and will are measured by the yardstick of their usual development. Remember that an untrained human voice has little effect on matter, but a trained operatic singer can shatter glass from the far side of a room. Similarly unexpected effects, some of them on a far more dramatic scale, show up as the potentials of the self are explored.

IMAGE AND INTERFACE: YESOD

The sphere of Yesod, called the Treasure House of Images, is the location of the intermediate realm that links the physical world and the inner realms. The images of Yesod can be vivid and seemingly objective—here, the polarization of subject and object is nearly as complete as it is in Malkuth—but they are not autonomous. They are vehicles for other energies and structured by other patterns. They are like emblems or icons in that they embody and express moods and ideas.

Any icon or emblem has a double quality: it is structured according to a set of conventions that allow it to represent ideas, and it arouses feelings that can serve as vehicles for more abstract energies.

The tarot trumps (and the pictures that are used in some decks for the Minor Arcana as well) are excellent examples of this. By now, you have probably gained some direct experience with the way in which the tarot emblems embody ideas and energies.

Attention to any image can provide access to these qualities, but those of the Yesod level, existing as they do as representations in consciousness without physical embodiments, are less polarized and thus less opaque. They serve as interfaces: that is, they are both instruments for detecting more inward, less concrete aspects of the cosmos, and tools for affecting or interacting with them. To construct an inward image is to work with structure and meaning. When you do it for a purpose, you build intention into it. When you attend to an inward image, you participate in its structure and thus—perhaps gradually, perhaps all at once—enter to some extent into its life.

So images are often felt to have power, and people often have an involuntary distaste for allowing their images to be "taken away" from them. Even aside from the question of photography or earlier methods of making images, people are sensitive about their appearance, and matters of grooming and appearance have been considered important in every society and at every period in history, even though the specifics vary rather widely. The power of the gaze is closely connected with the power of the image: being seen, for example, can be either a moment of vulnerability or a moment of triumphant self-assertion. To be invisible can be a kind of invulnerability, or the ultimate in isolation and rejection.

Working with images is a great part of magic, though not the only part. Magicians must be sensitive to images, enter into their lives and participate in the realms of being for which they serve as gates— not involuntarily, but at will. At the same time, they must learn to turn toward or away from image-consciousness at will, and not be a passive drifter on the tides of what 19th-century occultists and their followers called the astral light.

SYMBOLISM OF YESOD

As part of this lesson's work, you will learn a selection of the symbols traditionally assigned to the ninth sephirah. These are as follows:

Divine name: *ShDI AL ChI* (pronounced "Shah-dye ell Chye," with the "ch" pronounced as in "Bach")

Archangel: Gabriel, "Strength of God"

Angelic order: Kerubim, "Mighty Ones"

Astrological correspondence: Levanah, the Moon

Tarot correspondence: the four nines of the deck

As before, commit these correspondences to memory and write the first four into the four circles of Yesod on your Tree of Life diagram. Then color the rest of Yesod violet.

THE THIRTY-SECOND PATH

In this lesson, you will learn the basic symbolism of the last of the twenty-two paths of the Tree of Life, and practice it as before with the assistance of the corresponding tarot trump. The path and its symbolism are as follows:

Thirty-second path

Position on the Tree: Yesod to Malkuth

Hebrew letter: ת, Tau

Tarot correspondence: Trump XXI, the Universe

Astrological correspondence: Saturn

As you did in lesson 13, take some time to go back over the symbolism of the other paths and be sure that you have learned it thoroughly. You will have achieved the appropriate level of knowledge when a glance at the tarot card brings the path and its position, its Hebrew letter, and its astrological correspondence immediately to mind. That this may seem extreme or difficult is a commentary on the diminished sense of human capacities in today's society. You probably had this much mastery over the English alphabet by the time you finished first grade, after all, and gaining the same fluency with the symbolic alphabet of magic is unlikely to be beyond your abilities now.

READI₦G

Continue the reading practice from previous lessons. While reading your weekly chapter and selecting out the seven key sentences, concentrate on those that include or imply visual (or other sensory) images, and allow the images as well as the sentences themselves to form part of the furnishings of your mind during the day you spend on each.

Imaginary Journey Exercise

In practical magic, as suggested earlier, the trinity of will, imagination, and memory are essential and fundamental. There are countless ways to use these basic tools. One of the most common is the form of guided visualization often miscalled Pathworking, in which practitioners imagine themselves taking a journey through a visualized landscape bedecked with symbols of various kinds.

This form of working has been heavily overworked in many modern magical traditions, and it's not hard to find books that present either Pathworking or some particular set of Pathworkings as the ultimate key to magic. Nor is it hard to find books (some of which are the same books just mentioned) that present what is essentially a form of entertainment dressed up in the borrowed robes of magical practice. This differs from the recent flurry of fantasy movies only in that the visual effects are rarely up to Hollywood standards.

To give credit where it is due, guided visualization does have potential uses in magical training. It can function, when used intelligently, as a way to introduce novices to the imaginal realm and provide them with a framework for practice they can use later in more flexible ways. For those who don't or can't work with a magical lodge, guided visualizations of the right sort can replace some of the work of formal magical initiation, especially if the visualizations are carried out with intention and concentration, and repeated several times at least.

You need quite a bit of practice with the mechanics of magic, however, before any sort of guided visualization can have effects of this kind. Clear and solid imagery, along with intense and steady focus, go a long way toward making the most of these workings. Behind these lies the familiar need for the strong and skillfully aimed will.

The classic exercise of the imagined journey can help you develop the skills you need to work successfully with guided visualizations. Choose a trip that you frequently make on foot. It need not be very long, especially at first. If the longest distance you habitually walk is from your bedroom to the car on the street outside, this will do. Seated in your meditation posture, open with the usual gesture, and then imagine yourself making the journey you have chosen. Picture yourself moving at your usual speed from the starting point to the finish; see all the sights that surround you, whatever they happen to be. Bring in your other senses, so that you hear the usual sounds, smell the usual scents, feel the temperature of the air and the texture of the surface over which you walk.

As soon as convenient after the first time you make such an imaginary journey, make the same journey again physically, and pay careful attention to the sights, sounds, and other sensory experiences. Try to recall these and weave them into future imaginary journeys along the same route.

During the two weeks you spend on this lesson, do this exercise at least four times, using the same imagined journey each time. Note whether there is any improvement from the first session to the last. As always, keep notes on the experience in your magical journal.

SELF-PERCEPTION EXERCISE: INTUITION

The exercises of the last two lessons gave you some sense of how work with extended introspection proceeds. They also gave you a chance to see what sort of reactions you have to this aspect of magical practice. This, in itself, is a step in the direction of self-knowledge.

In this lesson, we turn the same process and the same state of background awareness toward a more elusive quarry. To the ninth sephirah is attributed the faculty of intuition, that odd and hard-to-define mode of knowing that provides insight from "out of the blue." Hunches and inspirations, instincts and creative flashes all fall into this category of perceptions. In today's culture, this side of human awareness receives a little lip service, but almost no attention. For this reason as well as others, many people have a certain amount of trouble telling intuitions from stray thoughts, unexplained feelings, or both. There is, however, one touchstone for all intuitive perceptions (albeit a subtle one)—the sense that the information coming through seems to come from outside the ordinary boundaries of the self.

Over the next two weeks, your task is to watch for the presence of intuition in your life. The same kind of "background watching" practiced in earlier phases of this exercise will be your most useful tool here. In your magical record, note down not only how successful you are at maintaining the background awareness and actually noticing intuitive perceptions, but also what sort of intuitions you get and how you respond to them.

TAROT: BEGINNING DIVINATION

The tarot exercises in lessons 12 and 13 introduced some of the basic skills used in the magical approach to tarot divination. The ability to balance the two aspects of that approach, the free play of imagery and the attentiveness to pattern, is something you will develop given time and regular practice.

The last five words of the above paragraph, as usual, are the most important. A student of the tarot armed with nothing but the deck itself (no books, no exercises, not even the little pamphlet of canned interpretations most decks contain) can easily become a skilled diviner through the simple process of dealing out one or a few cards to represent a given situation, seeing how the situation turns out, and comparing the event with the reading. This sort of feedback process is critical to the development of any kind of skill in divination. It requires only a willingness to learn from mistakes, which admittedly is not always the most common of commodities.

During the next two weeks, do the following simple divination exercise each day. Notice that it makes use of neither of the processes introduced in the last two lessons; this is deliberate. Those will be brought into play later. For now, your task is to try your hand at what amounts to bare intuition. For the sake of clarity, you may wish to do this exercise either first thing in the morning or last thing before you go to bed.

1. Sit in a comfortable position with your tarot deck in reach. Open with the usual gesture, then take the deck out of its container, hold it in your hands, and clear your mind of thoughts.

2. When your mind is reasonably quiet, say inwardly: *What one thing do I most need to understand about the next twenty-four hours?* Then shuffle the deck at least three times, and draw out a single card.

3. This card is the answer to your question. Examine it, think about it, turn it over in your mind, seeking some sense of what the answer means. When you have some notion of this—or when you decide you aren't going to find one—write down the card and the meaning you've found, and close with the usual gesture.

4. Just before you do the same exercise the next day, review the card, your interpretation, and the events of the day. What connections, if any, can you find? Make a note of anything you learn in your magical record.

Some students find this an easy practice; others find it difficult and frustrating. Whichever reaction you experience, pay attention to it, and take some time to think about why you've responded in this way.

MEDITATION

Continue with the system of meditation on symbols introduced in lesson 4. For the next two weeks, the topic for your meditation is the four nines of the tarot deck. As before, come up with a single word describing the meaning of each card as you understand it, then commit these words to memory.

Do this meditation each day during the two weeks you spend on this lesson. As always, enter a full description of your meditations in your magical record.

RITUAL

Perform the expanded Middle Pillar exercise given in lesson 11 each day during the two weeks you spend on this lesson. During this period, work on making the imagery of the exercise as bright and intense as possible. If you become aware of something in the practice that you can describe as "energy," concentrate on that as well. What seems to strengthen or weaken this part of the experience?

LESSON REVIEW

1. Perform the meditation as described above each day.
2. Perform the expanded Middle Pillar exercise as described above each day.

3. Perform the daily recollection each day on going to bed (see page 20).
4. Continue working with the reading exercise as described above.
5. Perform the will exercise described above.
6. Perform the self-perception exercise described above.
7. Perform the Tarot Divination exercise described above each day.
8. Continue working with the number exercise given in lesson 7.
9. Keep a record of your work.

When you have carried out this set of practices for at least two weeks, and have performed at least the minimum work listed above, you are ready to proceed to lesson 15.

LESSON 15

MAGIC AND DAILY LIFE

In this lesson, we complete the symbolic journey started in lesson 3, the descent of the Lightning Flash down the sephiroth of the Tree of Life. As Malkuth, the tenth sephirah, corresponds to the ordinary world of matter, this may be a good place to consider the interactions of these studies with the realm of everyday life.

There has been a great deal written about this interaction, much of it nonsense. Some magicians treat their art as though any contact with the ordinary world defiles it beyond repair. They hold up an ideal of the magician as a saintly hermit, utterly detached from the cares and desires of ordinary mortals. Others present magic as though its one purpose were to grant the fulfillment of every worldly desire to those too inept to manage this through ordinary means.

The tendency of Western culture to go to moral extremes in all things has warped thinking in this area far too much. Magicians in the West have always tended to be poor and socially marginal. The small number who have actually experienced any significant wealth or power is about the same in today's magical and Pagan community as it has been throughout Western history. Magicians' attitudes toward the material world have, therefore, tended toward longing or sour grapes, tempered with very little actual experience of fulfilled desire or worldly delights.

Here as elsewhere, the path between extremes tends to be the most useful. Although magicians interact with a wide range of levels and realms of being, they also must function in the same world as other human beings, a world in which rent must be paid and groceries bought, relationships built and children raised. Like any other realm of existence, this world has rules of its own that the magician may be able to use or circumvent, but cannot break. The mere fact of being a magician — that is, of having developed certain abilities in working with unfamiliar levels of existence — is no guarantee of success in the more familiar context of everyday life.

This said, it is nonetheless true that competence in magic can have a range of effects on the everyday world. It is equally true that the effects of practically oriented magic, if not carefully handled, can have unpleasant as well as positive consequences.

The successful use of ritual magic in any context depends on a clear grasp of the factors involved. This is not too difficult in a working involving, say, the astral level of being. Indeed, the forces at work on this level can be mapped out quite effectively using the Tree of Life. It is much harder, however, at the far greater complexity of the material level.

The difficulty becomes greater still when, as often happens, magicians don't understand their own motives, or have unresolved ambivalences toward their goals. Very often, the most important source of "external" problems is, in fact, internal. Most people's frustrations and sufferings are a function of their character rather than their circumstances. In fact, one of the more destructive outgrowths of human self-deception is that, the more loudly people blame the rest of the world for their troubles, the more likely it is that the actual difficulty lies within.

In such cases, ritual workings can easily backfire and produce outcomes quite different from the ones outwardly desired. This is the reason that ritual work tends to be far more successful when the person performing it has no emotional stake in the outcome. It is also the reason that initiates of traditional orders were normally urged to leave practical magic alone until they had achieved a certain level of self-knowledge and self-mastery.

This state of self-knowledge and self-mastery, the hallmark of the work of inner transformation, is anything but neutral in terms of the realm of ordinary life. On the one hand, the faculties of imagination, will, and memory are not precisely useless in everyday terms; a lack of one or another of these is responsible for a fair percentage of the total bulk of human misery in the world. On the other hand, self-knowledge and self-mastery are excellent weeding tools for removing the sort of internal conflicts, mixed motives, and ambivalences that cause so much failure in and out of a magical context. At the same time, both of these effects also build toward levels of maturity and perceptiveness at which practical magic, when it is appropriate, can be performed with success.

Magic is a much more complex matter than either fairy tales or modern media imagery would have it, and the results of magical training in terms of the everyday world partake of that complexity. Neither fantasies of omnipotence nor misunderstood notions of ascetic withdrawal are of much use in this context; common sense and recognition of both human fallibility and human potential have much more to offer.

MATTER AND MEANING: MALKUTH

Malkuth is the realm in which the polarization between subject and object is at its fullest. This is one reason why Malkuth is sometimes seen as a "fallen" version or aspect of Daath, the expression of the union of Chokmah and Binah, objectless wisdom and polarized understanding. In Daath, the primary polarity is horizontal, between powers on the same level of the Tree; in Malkuth, it is vertical. It is the realm in which the vision of the purely mechanical—process with no "inwardness"—becomes possible for the first time. (When Malkuth consciousness is carried back up the Tree, more abstract "mechanics" become conceivable.)

To beginning students of the Western magical traditions, Malkuth often seems to be something they should escape, or control, or transmute. The problem with this attitude is indicated by two very important, and all-too-often overlooked properties of Malkuth, summed up in these maxims: Malkuth sits on the throne of Binah, and Malkuth causes an influx to flow from the Prince of Countenances in Kether. But Malkuth is not merely the passive receptacle of all the other sephiroth. It has powers and effects of its own.

In one sense, Malkuth is the last sephirah to be emanated. In another, however, the whole sephirotic structure manifests outside time before it manifests in time. In a third sense, the entire Tree manifests simultaneously, and the sephiroth are interdependent. In a fourth sense, Malkuth and Kether are like the poles of a battery. It is their polarity that causes the current of manifestation to flow. This is why action and presence in Malkuth are so important magically. As long as we are alive, while we tread the path, we tread it in Malkuth. Our actions in Malkuth express inner forces, and govern and shape them as well.

To the extent that you go through life like a sleepwalker, simply drifting through experiences you make no attempt to understand or direct, you are passive to inner forces and express them unconsciously in your life and activities. To the extent that you act with conscious intention, you are awake, and your actions in Malkuth cause readjustments and realignments in the inner realms. You can find much to consider in the theme of "fourfoldness" that extends through all the sephiroth of the Middle Pillar. Malkuth may be the realm of the four elements, but those elements are rooted in the fourfold structure of Kether and its reflections down through the stations of the Middle Pillar.

This is one of the functions and prime magical uses of rules and regulations, and even of seemingly arbitrary prohibitions and requirements. They keep you from simply doing (or not doing) whatever it occurs to you to do or not do. They keep you from drifting along, and require that you make an effort. By making an effort, you come in some degree closer to awakening, to seeing, knowing, and acting—not in a dream, but in full consciousness. It is the practice of discrimination that teaches you to discern what is conducive to awakening and what to prolonging sleep.

In addition to intellectual and meditative practices, one of the most powerful tools of magical training is lodge work. There is a great deal of glamour attached to the idea of a magical lodge, but in fact some of the most powerful and important aspects of lodge work are the least glamorous and easiest to overlook. A lodge, magical or otherwise, is first and foremost a social form—that is, a structure through which certain kinds of relationships can be formed and maintained, and through which people can work together to achieve common ends. This is as true of magical lodges as it is of the most prosaic fraternal orders. The main difference between these two, perhaps, is that fraternal lodges generally handle structural issues with more competence than most of today's magical lodges, where mishandled energy often overwhelms inadequate structures.

The structures referred to here are not only the external, institutional structures as given in the constitution and bylaws. They are the internal structures built up (in the sphere of each member, and in the sphere of the lodge as a whole) through careful and conscientious participation in, and enactment of, lodge work.

An old saying has it that the true temple is the temple not made with hands, but built of living stones—that is, of the beings who have built themselves into the temple through their committed actions. This can easily be misunderstood, however. There is a certain phase of training, as there is in learning anything, in which students have to focus on the structures, and work and even struggle to assimilate them. But this is only a phase. The structures and procedures of the lodge are like grammar and syntax: they underlie all of speech and allow conversation to occur, but once they are grasped, they recede from consciousness. They are the vehicles of meaning, not meaning itself.

In the same way, the formal structures of lodge work are the vehicles of magical energy and transformation. They are not, by themselves, energy or transformation. Thus, pursuing the formal elements of lodge work while paying no attention to the inner, experiential dimension leads nowhere, just as a sentence can be grammatically and syntactically perfect and still communicate nothing, or nothing of interest. To discard them for that reason, however, is like discarding the grammar and syntax of ordinary language because it is a medium rather than a message. The result in either case is a drastic limitation in what can be accomplished.

SYMBOLISM OF MALKUTH

As part of this lesson's work, you will learn a selection of the symbols traditionally assigned to the tenth sephirah. These are as follows:

Divine name: *ADNI HARTz* (pronounced "Ah-doh-nye ha Ah-retz")

Archangels: Sandalphon, "Twin Brother," and Metatron (also archangel of Kether), Prince of Countenances

Angelic order: Ishim, humanity

Astrological correspondence: Olam Yesodoth, the sphere of the elements (the Earth)

Tarot correspondence: the four tens of the deck

As before, commit these correspondences to memory and write the first four into the four circles of Malkuth on your Tree of Life diagram. Then divide the rest of Malkuth into quarters, as shown in figure 14, with the upper quarter citrine (a yellowish brown), the left quarter russet, the right quarter olive green, and the bottom quarter black. (Alternatively, the whole can be colored dark green or black.)

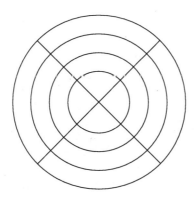

Figure 14. Malkuth divided.

READING

By now, you are accustomed to the reading exercise assigned earlier. It is now up to you to decide whether to continue it or not. If you choose to discontinue it, read at least two chapters in your current book during the two weeks you spend on this lesson. At the end of the two weeks, assess the differences, if any, in the amount you learned from those two chapters and the amount you learned from the chapters you worked through earlier.

WILL EXERCISE

Malkuth, the tenth sephirah, is, among other things, the sphere of the five ordinary senses. These can also be directed by the action of the will. In fact, they always are. Two people passing through the same set of events undergo entirely different experiences, in large part because of differences in the way their individual intentionalities shape what they perceive.

Many people are familiar with the more obvious expressions of this pattern. In one of his books, Tom Brown Jr., the well-known teacher of wilderness survival and outdoors awareness, tells of a group of people who went with him on a walk through the woods. At one point, he stopped and pointed to a patch of brush, asking the students what they saw. They readily identified the plant. He encouraged them to go closer and see what else they noticed. They went closer and reported that, yes, it was indeed the plant they had identified. He suggested that they go closer still. They were only a few feet away when the rabbit that had been sitting there, unnoticed by all of them, finally got up and hopped away.[1]

---

1. Tom Brown Jr., *Tom Brown's Field Guide to Nature Observation and Tracking* (New York: Berkley, 1983), p. 37.

Intentionality can also shape perception in many subtler ways. For the moment, however, just concentrate on this relatively basic mode. Like the people on the trail, you will pay attention to certain things. While this does not necessarily require you to ignore others, the experience can be enlightening!

On four different times during the two weeks you spend on this lesson, take a walk through an area you know moderately well. Follow the same route each time. Immediately before each walk, decide on one thing that will be the target of the exercise—a color or a common object, for example. Choose at least one that involves a sense other than vision. For example, you may choose to spend one walk paying attention to the sounds of voices. Your goal is to find as many examples of your target as possible.

If you choose to spend one walk focusing on red things, notice as many of them as possible. Keep a running total; if this is difficult for you, bring a notepad and a pen and make a tally mark each time you spot something red. Challenge yourself to find as many of them as possible. It may take some effort at first, but after a while, you are likely to find red things leaping out at you from the background.

It's important, for the sake of this exercise, to have only one target in mind during each walk. That is why we ask you to choose the actual target immediately before the walk. Pay attention to your experiences during each walk.

SELF-PERCEPTION EXERCISE: SYNTHESIS

The self-perception exercises over the last three lessons have given you a clearer idea of how you habitually deal with three different aspects of your consciousness. They have also helped you develop a certain specific tool of awareness, one with broad uses in certain kinds of magical work.

More broadly, however, they have had another purpose. The "background awareness" they teach is one form of a more general state that has been called, in a number of different spiritual and magical traditions, "detachment." Detachment is the ability to draw back at least slightly from the monkey antics of ordinary consciousness and make them objects of consciousness in their own right.

A common metaphor in esoteric writings describes the state of awareness usual to human beings as a kind of dreaming. In the ordinary dream state, consciousness becomes completely submerged in the phantasmagoria of the dream; no matter how bizarre or contradictory the events perceived, the dreaming mind accepts them unquestioningly. Nightmare monsters that seem ludicrous to the waking mind are objects of paralyzing terror in their dream context.

The same is too often true of your ordinary waking state. People become submerged in the events, the emotions, the opinions and reactions of everyday life as thoroughly as any dreamer in a dream. Contradictions, delusive hopes and fears, and a horde of other nightmare creatures as bizarre as anything in dreams take the place of a clear perception of the inner and outer universe.

Recently, a number of psychologists have gained some publicity with books and articles about "lucid dreaming"—that rare class of dream in which the dreamer becomes conscious of the dream state while it is still going on, and can therefore shape the dream at will. While such dreams can have a place within certain kinds of esoteric work, a far more important state is one we might call "lucid waking." Just as lucid dreaming involves being aware of the nature of the dream state and, thus, being able to shape it, lucid waking involves being aware of the nature of ordinary waking consciousness, and, in the same way, being able to transform it at will.

This is much of what lies behind the common understanding of magic. Just as a lucid dreamer can shape dream-stuff, so the "lucid waker" (the magician, in more traditional terms) shapes the raw material of waking consciousness. There is this difference between the two, of course: a dream is a private experience, while waking consciousness is at least partly built up collectively by families, communities, and entire cultures.

It is thus important to realize that, in reshaping their own experience of the world, magicians have an effect on the experience of others. There are ethical consequences to this, as there are to anything that affects other people. There are also practical consequences. The people affected by a magician's actions may not respond positively to those actions, even (or especially) when such actions are "positive" from the magician's point of view. History suggests that negative reactions are a good deal more likely. These negative reactions can be propelled by fear to a lethal intensity and, too often, to a lethal conclusion.

All these considerations are involved in the process of detachment, of the consciousness-of-consciousness these self-perception exercises teach. The last exercise helps you explore some of their implications in your own life.

The method here will be the same as in the last three exercises. You will use the "background awareness" discussed earlier to monitor an aspect of your life. In this case, however, the topic is more closely focused.

Your goal is to become aware of how your current magical practices affect your interactions with other people. Some of these effects may be obvious: you may have arranged with family or housemates for private time for practices, and altered their daily schedules as a result. Others will be subtle. Watch for them, and keep track of what you find.

The list of motives for magical practice you developed in lesson 10 can be useful here. Each of these motives is likely to be linked to specific actions, and these to specific effects. Work on being aware of this for the next two weeks. As always, keep notes on your discoveries in your magical record.

TAROT DIVINATION

You have gained some sense of the way you relate to the cards in a divinatory context from two weeks of practice with the simple form of divination given in lesson 14. Now it's time to combine that simple form with the skills practiced earlier into a more complete method of divinatory work.

For the next two weeks, do the following daily divination exercise. As before, it may be easiest to do it at the beginning or end of your day.

1. Sit at or on a convenient flat surface, with your tarot deck within reach. Open with the usual gesture, take the deck from its container, and hold it in your hands.
2. After quieting your mind, say inwardly: *What do I most need to understand about the next twenty-four hours?*
3. Shuffle the deck at least three times, divide it in half, and draw three cards, one at a time, from the top of the lower half. Turn them over as you draw them, and set them in a line from left to right in front of you.
4. These three cards give the answer to your question. That answer is a story, told in the images, people, and situations

shown in the three cards. The cards can be seen as the story's beginning, middle, and end. The answer is also a sequence of elemental symbols that may conflict, reinforce, or harmonize, and these interactions should be reflected in the plot of the story.

5. Try to summarize the story in a sentence or two; for example, the sequence King of Wands/Five of Wands/Tower may be summarized as, "A fiery and willful person gets involved in a large-scale fight, which ends with everything in a wreck." Take this summary and think about the situations and people you expect to encounter during the next twenty-four hours. In particular, think about how well any court cards relate to your own personality. In the example just given, for instance, you may find it useful to assess your own temper, and to consider reining it in for a day or two!

6. Once you have finished, write down the card, the story, and any ideas you may have about its meaning, then close with the usual gesture.

7. As before, review the first divination before you move on to another, and try to determine to what in your day's experience it related. Write down your perceptions.

You will continue this exercise through the next lesson, so it's not necessary to get results in a hurry. Simply do the exercise and see what results appear. Comparing the events of the day to the divination will gradually teach you how to make sense of the play of symbols. The result is likely to express itself as a unique and personal understanding of the cards, but this is in no way a disadvantage.

MEDITATION

Continue with the system of meditation on symbols introduced in lesson 4. For the next two weeks, the topic for your meditation is the four tens of the tarot deck. As before, come up with a single word describing the meaning of each card as you understand it, then commit these words to memory.

Do this meditation each day during the two weeks you spend on this lesson. As always, enter a full description of your meditations in your magical record.

RITUAL

Perform the expanded Middle Pillar exercise given in lesson 11 each day during the two weeks you spend on this lesson. Review the instructions to be sure of your grasp of the details, and for the next two weeks try to raise each aspect of this practice—imagery, energy, mental focus, intensity of effort, perceived effect—to the highest pitch you can achieve. Keep notes on the results in your magical record.

LESSON REVIEW

1. Perform the meditation each day as described above.
2. Perform the expanded Middle Pillar exercise each day as described above.
3. Perform the daily recollection each day upon going to bed (see page 20).
4. Perform this lesson's self-perception exercise as described above.

5. Either continue the reading exercise, or discontinue it and read two chapters from your text in the ordinary way.

6. Perform the will exercise described above four times.

7. Perform the Tarot Divination exercise described above each day.

8. Complete working with the number exercise given in lesson 7.

9. Keep a record of your work.

When you have practiced these exercises for at least two weeks, and done at least the minimum work listed above, you are ready to proceed to lesson 16.

LESSON 16

THE MAGICAL LODGE

With the last three lessons of this course, we shift the focus and direction of study one last time. In previous lessons, we portrayed the work of the magician-in-training as a largely solitary project, a process of personal transformation carried out by individuals through their own studies and practical work.

This picture contains a good deal of truth. At the same time, there are also collective aspects of magic—directions and types of study and practice, and levels of development that come out of magical work carried out in a group context. Magical development always depends on the foundation of solitary work; no amount of group rituals, initiations, or other activities can make up for neglecting the essential, and essentially solitary, work of personal transformation. While it's entirely possible to reach the goals of magic on a wholly solitary basis, however, there are many benefits to magical group work as well.

Let's look again at how a person learns to play a musical instrument. A great deal of the work involved is personal and best done in privacy, particularly in the early stages, so you can make mistakes and work through your initial awkwardness with a minimum of embarrassment. It's entirely possible for a musician to spend his or her entire musical career as a solo artist. At the same time, some levels of musicianship and some kinds of music can only be experienced by working together with other musicians. The experience of community and the expansion of the sometimes overly narrow boundaries of the self that unfolds from participating in a common project is another major advantage. For musicians (and magicians), feedback and instruction from more experienced masters can speed up your learning process and help you avoid certain mistakes and dead ends.

THE MAGICAL LODGE

The traditional structure of working groups among magicians in the West is the magical lodge. Derived from the medieval guild system by way of Freemasonry and other fraternal lodge organizations, and adapted to occult use by a succession of 18th- and 19th-century magical orders, the lodge system was the standard method of group organization in the Western esoteric tradition from the 18th century to the beginning of the modern occult renaissance in the 1960s. Even at the present time, most traditional magical groups around the Western world use some variant of it.

What is a magical lodge? Answers abound, depending on perspective. From a practical standpoint, however, a magical lodge is a group of magicians who:

1. *Meet regularly for working purposes:* This first point is critical. A magical lodge is not merely a study group, or a network for support or the exchange of ideas (although it may be these things in addition to its other functions). If it is worth the

name, it has regular meetings at which rituals and other magical exercises are performed. This provides space and time for the development of the group dimensions of magic mentioned earlier.

2. *Have an established organizational and leadership structure:* Abuses of power at many levels of our society have produced (particularly in the countercultural circles where so many magicians are found) a distrust of all organized systems. Unfortunately, nature abhors a power vacuum as much as any other kind; experiments in unorganized magical working groups have tended either to disintegrate or to become de facto dictatorships centered around one or two charismatic members. In a lodge system, by contrast, lodge members fill a series of offices with specific roles and responsibilities, and rotate from office to office at intervals, while a set of general rules (comparable to a constitution) provides a framework for the whole process. The result, when it works, is a framework where organizational needs are taken care of with minimal fuss, and as much time and energy as possible are reserved for the magical work that is the lodge's reason for existence.

3. *Admit only lodge members to their meetings:* This habit has led to charges of elitism among magical lodges, charges that have sometimes been well founded. Historically, this habit has been largely a function of the persecution of magic, which (at least at the moment) is in abeyance in most of the Western world. Still, there are valid reasons for a working group to limit its meetings to its own members. Many forms of group work require a high degree of training and experience among participants. Bringing in the general public—some of whom may have no background at all in magic, others who may have radically

different ideas about how ritual work should be done—is an effective way to bring about confusion and failure or, alternatively, to limit what can be done to the lowest common denominator. In the same way, professional sports teams and theatrical companies don't usually invite members of the audience to join them in their performances. On the other hand, these groups do have audiences, while magic is not a spectator sport.

4. *Offer one or more initiations to members:* This is, in many ways, the heart of the magical lodge system. The subject of initiation will be discussed in more depth later, but for now we can define an initiation as a group ritual designed to assist the personal, spiritual, and/or magical development of one member of the group. Most magical lodges have a series of such rituals that are passed through in a specific order and bring about specific kinds of transformation in their participants. Most often, the first such initiation is also used to bring new members formally into the lodge, while other initiations may have roles in the lodge's organizational structure. For example, there may be offices that can only be held by a member who has received a certain level of initiation.

5. *Use some elements of traditional lodge culture:* It is rarely recognized by people who have not had the experience of belonging to a fraternal or magical lodge that lodges are the inheritors of a substantial collection of practices, tools, symbolism, ritual, art, and architecture—in fact, an entire culture that is largely consistent between different lodge organizations. This consistency shows itself in small ways. For example, three raps with a gavel will bring the members to their feet in most lodge organizations currently active in North

America. This consistency appears in broader contexts as well. These similarities, however, are beyond the scope of this course.[2] Membership in a working lodge, of course, brings with it an introduction to the elements of lodge culture that are part of that lodge's particular toolkit of methods.

In the remaining lessons, we will discuss certain other features of the lodge system, including the role of secrecy in magical groups and the nature and function of initiation. We will not give specific examples from the workings of particular magical orders, but will cover material generally applicable to the lodges of most magical orders. If you choose to join a magical lodge—which, of course, you may or may not do—you will soon discover how much of the material covered in this course can be applied to the particular lodge organization in which you find a place.

COURSE REVIEW

This lesson begins the final unit of our course, and a survey of some of what you've learned is helpful here.

In the last fifteen lessons, you learned some of the basic concepts of the Western esoteric tradition, including the different levels of being, the use of symbolism, the role of energy, the structure of the self, and the problems and possibilities involved in magical training. You acquired certain basic methods of magical practice, including meditation, the Lesser Banishing Ritual of the Pentagram, the Middle Pillar exercise, and the use of the tarot deck. You explored some of

---

2. For other sources on the subject, see John Michael Greer, *Inside a Magical Lodge* (St. Paul, MN: Llewellyn, 1998).

the symbolism and meaning of the Tree of Life, and of the Qabalistic philosophy from which it derives. You also tackled a series of tests and challenges designed to develop self-knowledge.

Learning all of this material, in turn, presupposes a willingness on your part to work with it, think about it, make use of it. Your willingness may have increased and decreased according to time and circumstances, and this is to be expected. In magic, as in anything else, there are no perfect students! There may have been times over the last thirty weeks when your studies and practices went easily, and others when they went with difficulty, if at all. There may be gaps in your journal when no practices were done, or where they were done but never written down. There may be parts of the lessons you found difficult, confusing, or offensive, but you can put such difficulties to use.

During the next two weeks, read through the complete series of lessons, from 1 to 15. Make a note of any parts of the lessons, whether theoretical or practical, that were difficult for you. In particular, note any practice you did only occasionally, or did not do at all. Once you have completed this review, consider the parts of the work that were difficult for you, and see what common elements or qualities they may have. What do these common factors say about your approach to magical training, or to high magic as you understand it?

Note down in your practice journal anything you discover.

WILL EXERCISE

Over the previous weeks and months, we introduced a series of exercises for exploring, strengthening, and clarifying the will. There were entire books of such exercises published in the late 19th and early 20th centuries, although few magicians are aware of them at present.

It would be easy for us to continue passing on specific exercises during the last lessons of this course.

On the other hand, there is much to be said for individual initiative, and these final lessons are well suited to stress this point. Your assignment during the two weeks you spend on this lesson is to come up with a will exercise of your own. If you wish, you may simply modify one of the earlier exercises, or you may come up with something wholly original. Either way, design it, do it at least four times over the next two weeks, and keep notes on the experience in your magical journal.

MEDITATION

The meditations given in lesson 15 completed the sequence of workings on the Tree of Life begun in lesson 4. By now, you've had the opportunity to work with the symbolism of each of the first ten numbers at a basic level and, in the process, to learn something about one of the central methods of meditation in the Western esoteric tradition.

Now, apply this same method in a more flexible and more personally directed way. In the course of your reading and study, you have no doubt come across many different points that did not make sense to you, or that seemed to be saying more than you felt you were hearing. Your first task is to identify several of these; the course review discussed above is likely to be helpful in this connection.

Once you have several points that roused your curiosity or caused you perplexity, select one and use it as the focus for one or more sessions of meditation. You may find that it takes more than a single session to make sense of the point you are trying to explore; you may also find that one point, even when clarified, leads to others that would benefit from further meditation. Direct your meditations as seems best to you.

In each practice session, after the usual opening process, focus your attention as intensely as possible on the subject of the meditation, visualizing it if it is best represented by an image, repeating it silently several times if it is best represented by words. Then think about it in general terms for a while, choose one aspect of the subject that seems promising, and focus your thoughts on it, pursuing it as far as you can. As always, if your thoughts stray from the subject, bring them gently back to it and continue.

Mastering this art, the art of discursive meditation, is among the most important steps you can take toward the attainment of magical knowledge and abilities. As you develop the capacity to unfold the meanings of magical texts and symbols in meditation, you will find a great deal of information available to you that can be obtained in no other way.

Notice, as you continue with your meditations, that some elements of this practice overlap with the method of focused reading covered earlier in this course. In particular, you may find it valuable to experiment with the habit of selecting the topic for meditation before going to bed each night, studying it at that time, sleeping on it, and then exploring it in meditation the next morning. You can also bring other skills developed in the course of the reading exercise into play as you see fit.

ÍΠΠER-PLAΠE WORKÍΠG

In lesson 14, you visualized a journey as a will exercise. We mentioned at that point that it could be used as the basis for important magical developments. Now, we will provide a way into one of the most important of these developments—inner-plane working.

The key to this method is the combination of meditative and ritual modes of practice. This combination is the key to most of the methods used in full-scale magical practice, by magical lodges as well as by solitary practitioners. The following exercise will help you explore this kind of working.

1. Prepare your practice space by putting a chair facing east in the center of the area in which you usually perform your ritual work.

2. Make the opening gesture, and then perform the Lesser Banishing Ritual of the Pentagram in the usual way (see page 51). Stand directly behind the chair at those phases in which you would normally stand in the center.

3. When you have finished the banishing, sit down on the chair and begin the relaxation and breathing work you normally do at the beginning of a meditation.

4. When this is completed, turn your attention to the Tiphareth center at your heart. Visualize this as a golden sphere of light, just as you would in the Middle Pillar exercise. Focus on this for a time, and then visualize the sphere of light expanding outward in all directions. Allow your awareness of your physical surroundings to fade out as the sphere expands to the size of a large room.

5. From your heart center, visualize the image of a magical lodge or temple expanding outward until its corners nearly touch the boundaries of the sphere. The lodge is a room fashioned in a perfect cube, with height, length, and width identical. The walls, floor, and ceiling are of pale golden stone. At the center is a cubical altar covered with a black cloth. In the center of each wall is a doorway, and a few feet in front of each doorway is an empty throne. The doorways themselves are closed by curtains,

each of which bears the image of a tarot ace: ahead of you, in the east, a yellow curtain with the Ace of Swords; behind you, in the west, a blue curtain with the Ace of Cups; to your right, a red curtain with the Ace of Wands; to your left, a green curtain with the Ace of Pentacles. There is also a skylight above the altar, and clear light streams down through it. You yourself are sitting in a chair facing east, halfway between the altar and the western wall of the room. (See figure 15 for a map of the room.)

For the first two times you work on this exercise, stop at this point and mentally go over each detail of the image, building it up in your mind's eye as clearly as possible for the period of time you've set aside for your meditation. When the meditation is at an end, go to step 9 of this exercise and proceed from there.

After these first two repetitions, continue on from here to step 6.

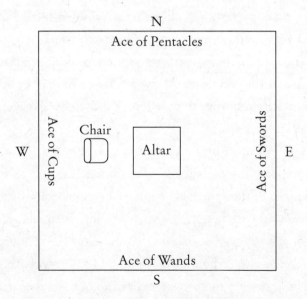

Figure 15. Map of the visualized lodge room.

6. Visualize yourself rising to your feet within the lodge room
   you have built up. (Your physical body remains in its seat.)
   Move around the lodge, slowly at first; your visualized body
   should move and function in exactly the same way that your
   physical one does. When you are comfortable moving in the
   visualized temple (this may take a short time, or several
   sessions), go on to the next step.

7. Go to the west of the altar in your visualized body and face
   east. Beginning there, without making any physical movements
   or sounds, perform the Lesser Invoking Ritual of the
   Pentagram. This is identical to the banishing ritual (see page
   51), except that you trace the pentagram differently (see figure
   16 below). The banishing pentagrams are not used inside an
   inner-plane temple of this sort, since this would disperse the
   energetic forms you are constructing.

   When visualizing the four archangels, imagine them seated
   in the thrones, and try to perceive the feeling or quality of each
   element present in the appropriate quarter of the room.

8. Return to the chair. Then, slowly, visualize the lodge room

Begin here

Figure 16. Invoking pentagram.

contracting back into your solar-plexus center. When you have
done this, bring the sphere of light back into yourself as well,
reversing the process of opening. Hold the image of the
Tiphareth sphere for a moment, and then allow it to fade.
Finally, close the practice as usual for a meditation.

The complete temple structure must always be withdrawn back
into yourself at the end of each practice session. Since it is formed
out of the substance of your astral body, leaving it externalized can
bring about exhaustion and a range of health problems.

Perform this practice at least four times during the two weeks
you spend on this lesson. Eight times is probably a reasonable maximum. If you find yourself feeling unsteady, dizzy, or disconnected
from the ordinary world after performing a session, eat a meal as
soon as possible to help yourself return to ordinary states of consciousness, and wait at least three days before repeating the exercise.

TAROT DIVINATION

For the next two weeks, continue with the tarot divination exercise
introduced in lesson 15. In reviewing each day's reading, try to find
the specific meanings of each tarot symbol in terms of the day's events.
Note what kinds of events each type of symbol seems to represent
most often; if you find no such repeating patterns, note this also.
Incorporate what you learn into your interpretations of the cards.

THE MIDDLE PILLAR EXERCISE: SECOND EXPANSION

The Middle Pillar exercise, in a variety of forms, has been a part of
your daily practices now for several months. As part of your review,

take the time to go back over the practices you've done. Notice whether they seem to have developed in any particular way, and if so, how.

Now let's add another element—a circulation of energies coordinated with your breath. Add this only after you have drawn energies from above and below and stabilized them at the Tiphareth center at your heart, but before you perform the final Qabalistic Cross.

1. Once the energies are stabilized at your heart center, draw in a breath, and imagine the breath flowing into your Tiphareth center, blending with the golden energy there.
2. Still breathing in, lead the current of energy out to your left side and down the outside of your body and your left leg, all the way to the Malkuth center between your feet.
3. Pause, holding your breath. Then, breathing out, allow the current of energy to flow up from your Malkuth center, up the outside of your right leg and your body to the level of your heart, where it flows back inward to the Tiphareth center. The light remains there, while your breath continues up and out through your nostrils.
4. When you have finished breathing out, hold the breath out for a time, then begin again with an inhalation.

Repeat this entire process four times. It is common practice to time the stages of your breath using the same fourfold rhythm you use to prepare for meditation. Thus, if you are using the fourfold breath, draw the breath in and the current of light down to your feet, counting to four; hold, counting to four; let the current of light rise back up to your heart, and breathe out, counting to four. Hold the breath out, counting to four. Once you have completed the cycle of energies four times, do the final Qabalistic Cross and close (see pages 38 and 15).

LESSON REVIEW

1. Meditate each day.
2. Perform the daily recollection each day on going to bed (see page 20).
3. Perform the Middle Pillar exercise each day in the expanded form, with the new final phase introduced in this lesson.
4. Perform the Tarot Divination exercise described above each day.
5. Begin the course review as described above.
6. Perform the will exercise as described above.
7. Perform the inner-plane working as described above four to eight times.
8. Keep a record of your work.

When you have carried out these exercises for at least two weeks and have performed at least the minimum required work, you are ready to proceed to lesson 17.

LESSON 17

THE MYSTERIES
OF MAGIC

Any magician working in the milieu of the current occult renaissance has the responsibility to choose from among a wide range of traditional and modern practices, teachings, and approaches to the world. In many cases, the choices are straightforward, but certain decisions involve a broad range of issues. One relates to the way Western magical traditions have habitually interacted with the society around them.

Here the Western esoteric tradition differs sharply from its partial equivalents in other cultures—the shamanic systems of tribal peoples, for instance, or the esoteric schools of great Eastern faiths such as Buddhism and Taoism. These traditions, past and present, play active parts in their respective cultures, with well-defined and highly visible social roles. In the West, by contrast, occult traditions have existed on the fringes of society, usually as a part-time activity of people who must earn their living in some other way.

Western magical traditions tend to be as secretive as possible. This secrecy has been so pervasive that one common term for the esoteric realm of knowledge—the occult—literally means "hidden."

For the last two centuries, many magicians have spoken of the entire body of magical lore as "the Mysteries," a term that also implies a high degree of secrecy, or at least confusion.

SECRECY AND MAGIC

In every culture, the magician exists in a border zone, a space between the socially constructed world and the unknown. Some societies establish a special occupation (such as "shaman") for those who inhabit this zone and value them; others declare the zone a no-man's land and do their best to punish or kill those who set foot in it. American culture at present does neither. Pulled between incompatible systems of thought—science, which sees magic as crazy; orthodox religions, which see it as evil; alternative religions, which see it as possible; and folk belief, which has always assumed its existence and power—our society has yet to come up with a generally accepted way to define the zone and react to its inhabitants.

To some extent, this gives today's magicians an unusual freedom, the freedom to define their own place and role in the world. It may be inappropriate, however, to celebrate this too much, or too soon. Similar periods of social uncertainty have come and gone before.

Traditionally, magicians in the West have tended to practice their art at a level of secrecy more generally associated with espionage or organized crime. False names, passwords and signs, and blood oaths came into common use in Western magical traditions in this way. These things were necessary in the days when even the suspicion of magical involvement could lead to torture and death; they continued to be useful later, when such a suspicion was enough to destroy careers and risk criminal charges or confinement for insanity.

Today, in an age where religious freedom is perhaps more general than ever before in history, this level of security seems excessive. There have accordingly been a number of recent figures in the magical community who have roundly condemned the whole apparatus of traditional magical secrecy. A point can be made for this, as there have been some significant abuses of the traditional secrecy of magic.

Aleister Crowley commented bitterly of his initiation into the Hermetic Order of the Golden Dawn, in which he was sworn to secrecy by bloodcurdling oaths and then presented with the Hebrew alphabet, the symbols of the planets, and several other widely available bits of occult lore. The Golden Dawn did, as it happens, have material to offer its higher grades that was unavailable outside its doors; the same has not been true of every magical lodge. Less pleasant are those situations, uncommon but by no means unknown, where the traditional secrecy of magic was used as a cover for various kinds of fraud, illegal activities, or political conspiracy.

At the same time, there is something to be said for some of the technical devices of security that have become part of the tradition during the long years of hiding. The methods used for security in Western magical circles, particularly in the magical orders of the last 300 years, have taken on unexpected roles in esoteric practice. Thus the idea of taking a false name, sensible enough in its own context, has developed into the custom of choosing a magical name or motto to express personal aspirations in magic. Passwords have taken on some of the functions of mantras; secret grips, used by lodge members to identify each other, have come to be used as a way of linking energy prior to a group working. Over and above their function as a means of ensuring secrecy, these are effective magical techniques, and worth using in their own right.

There are also good reasons for a magician to choose to be quiet about his or her interests and practice, even now. Some of these are psychological: the sense of isolation and focus created by a secret rigorously held can be a valuable tool for the magician in the work of transformation. So can the taming of the ego involved in not parading your status as a magician before all your friends and acquaintances.

Other reasons are purely pragmatic. Although involvement in esoteric work is acceptable, even fashionable, in some countercultural circles, the levels of ignorance about magic in our culture as a whole are high enough to create suspicion and confused communication even when religious zealotry doesn't enter the picture. There are still parts of the United States where it is not physically safe to be known as a practitioner of magic. Moreover, despite the optimism of some factions of the magical community, it cannot be assumed that the opposition to magic in our culture will necessarily grow feebler with the passage of time.

Twenty-five years ago, the idea that antiabortion sentiment might lead to the firebombing of clinics and the murder of doctors would have seemed outlandish even to the most radical of abortion-rights activists. Similarly, it's not impossible that religious opposition to the current renaissance of magical traditions may take on increasingly militant and violent forms. It is even possible that the current broad tolerance for alternative spirituality in our culture may give way to more repressive attitudes. At the moment, neither of these seems especially likely, but predicting the future is always the riskiest of magical arts.

THE ART OF SECRECY

Finally, there is an esthetic of secrecy within the Western esoteric tradition, a part of the culture of Western magic that has come to use secrecy, invisibility, and elusiveness as a kind of artistic medium. This is especially important in the culture of the lodge tradition, discussed briefly in lesson 16. Lodges of all kinds, perhaps more than any other group in the modern Western world, have treated secrecy as an art form in ways that are often playful.

Thus, for example, many of the buildings constructed by fraternal lodge organizations have exteriors that deliberately mislead the viewer about the layout of the internal rooms—hallways, for instance, seem to lead somewhere in particular, but actually go around in a circle or right out onto the street through another door. A hundred years ago, similarly, lodge members were coached in secret signs of recognition to use with other lodge members, even though most people who belonged to lodges made no secret of their involvement.

All this may seem reminiscent of the sort of make-believe games that lead children to pretend to be pirates or cowboys, and inspire adults to dress up like Star Trek® characters and say "Beam me up, Scotty" into plastic communicators. There is, however, more to it than that. Secrecy is a powerful form of training of the will. Human beings are social and communicative creatures. Having to keep something absolutely secret from anyone other than the members of a lodge requires, not only a noticeable effort of will, but a good deal of attentiveness in order not to give away the secret by accident.

There are other, deeper aspects of secrecy in a magical setting. These unfold from the role of secrecy as a symbol of those levels of experience hidden, by their very nature, from the unawakened mind. These cannot be revealed except by being re-veiled. As you pursue your magical training, you will need to work your way through the issues of secrecy. If you decide to seek membership in a lodge, you will almost certainly be asked to pledge yourself to secrecy regarding the teachings and business of the lodge. Usually the names and personal information of members are covered by the same pledge. Don't take this obligation lightly. Once you take it, keep it strictly.

COURSE REVIEW

Lesson 16's work included a review as one part of the summing-up process that is so important in this final unit of the course. In this lesson, you'll be continuing that process in a slightly different way.

Your task over the next two weeks is to read through your magical record, starting with your first work on lesson 1 and finishing with your most recent entries. Notice the changes in the central practices of the course—meditation, the banishing ritual, etc. Pay attention as well to any changes you may perceive in the tone of the entries, and in your attitude to magic they express.

As always, note anything you learn in your magical record.

SECRECY EXERCISE

The theme of secrecy has long had a major role in Western magical traditions. As you move toward the completion of this course, explore your own attitudes toward secrets and secrecy. Set aside an hour or so when you will not be interrupted, and provide yourself with paper and a pen or pencil. Your goal is to make four lists: one that enumerates things about yourself that you feel comfortable discussing with anyone in the world, one that contains things about yourself that you prefer not to talk about except with people you know, one that includes things about yourself that you only discuss with one person or a few specific individuals, and that records things about yourself that you would prefer never to discuss with anyone at all.

When you have finished making the lists, examine them and see what patterns you can find. Are there particular aspects of your life that you would rather keep secret, and others that you feel more comfortable sharing with others? Why is that?

When you are finished, destroy all four lists so there is no possibility anyone can read them. Does this action set off any emotional reactions? If so, what are they?

As before, note down the practice and your reactions to it in your magical journal.

WILL EXERCISE

By now, you have practiced an extended series of exercises meant to develop what magicians call the lower will, the capacity of the self to choose its direction and intentionality consciously. One goal of this training is to develop strength and clarity of will, and the ability to focus that will into magical rituals and other forms of practical work. Will and imagination, as many of the standard books of magic point out, are the essential tools of magical practice. Magicians imagine a goal richly and fully, direct their will toward it with maximum strength and intensity, and reap the results.

This same pattern, however, is equally applicable to the many aspects of life that do not seem magical at all, in the ordinary sense of the word. The sustained use of imagination and will can transform your life and reshape your surroundings even if none of the technical methods of magic are put to use.

In reality, of course, there is nothing that is not magical. The lower and higher wills are not two separate things in any ultimate sense, and so any action that expresses imagination and will is a magical action. Your task in this lesson, and after you have finished this course entirely, is to put this realization to work in your own life.

It was once customary in the literature on will training to talk about the unlimited potential of work of this kind. While this is accurate up to a point, remember that nine months of study and practice will not transform you into an adept. As you consider the possibilities of willed, imaginative action in your own life, keep a sense of proportion and remember that subtle changes carried out with firmness and persistence usually accomplish more than grand projects of a scale you may not be able to sustain.

Your assignment for this lesson is to change some aspect of your life using the tools you have already learned and whatever degree of power and clarity of will you have achieved. Select an aspect of your life that is unsatisfactory and improve it. Or choose to change something arbitrary, like a harmless habit. In either case, select a goal, go to work, and note down your experiences and results in your magical journal.

MEDITATION

Continue using the developed approach to meditation introduced in lesson 16 during the time you spend on this lesson. Your course review is likely to prove a significant source of topics for meditation. Another source, one that was hinted at in the discussion in lesson 16, can be found in the books on magic you study. Between these two sources, you should be able to find more than enough to keep your meditations occupied.

INNER-PLANE WORKING

The method of inner-plane working covered in lesson 16 represents a first step toward a wide range of magical techniques. The fusion of meditative and ritual actions in a visualized context is central to a large part of the work of the modern magician. At the same time, some of the skills developed by this kind of exercise also play a central role in other types of magical working, notably the method of visionary work traditionally called "scrying in the spirit vision," but more often known at present under the usually inaccurate label of "Pathworking."

Most of these developments of the method lie outside the scope of this book. Many are covered in detail in books currently in print. The work for this lesson expands on the material given in lesson 16 and adds to the foundations already laid there. The same material will be expanded further in lesson 18 and used as the basis for the ceremony of self-initiation that will be presented at the end of this course.

1. Begin, as in last lesson's meditation, by banishing the space and entering into meditation, projecting the sphere of light and the lodge within the sphere from your solar-plexus center.

2. Perform the Lesser Invoking Ritual of the Pentagram (see page 233) in a visualized body. At the conclusion of this process, you are standing in the midst of a visualized magical lodge, with the four archangels present in the four thrones.

3. For the first two sessions you devote to this exercise, remain at the altar, facing east, still in your visualized body. Then, perform the Middle Pillar exercise in that body. The Lesser Banishing Ritual of the Pentagram should not be done in this setting; simply begin with the Qabalistic Cross (see page 38), and then start formulating the energy centers in the usual way. During this process, make no physical movement or sound; do everything in visualization. When the exercise is finished, go on to step 4.

4. For the remaining sessions you devote to this exercise, the work will be rather different. At the beginning of each of these sessions, when you first visualize the lodge, include in the visualization a silver goblet standing at the center of the altar. When you go over to the altar to begin the invoking ritual, be aware that the goblet is filled with clear water. Then, at the conclusion of the invoking ritual, remain at the altar, facing east. Still in your visualized body, raise your hands outward and up, above your head, and look upward toward the skylight above the altar. Say:

Come in the power of the Light;
Come in the Light of Wisdom;
Come in the mercy of the Light;
The Light hath healing in its wings!

5. Visualize a brilliant ray of light descending through the skylight to the goblet, shining on cup and water with blinding intensity. Hold this image for a time, and then allow the ray of light to fade.

6. Take the goblet in both hands, raise it to your lips, and drink some of the water. Try to imagine the taste and feeling of the cool water as clearly as possible as your visualized body drinks. Set the goblet down, leaving it partly full, and go on to Step 7.

7. With the work of the meditation done, return to your seat and your physical body. Withdraw the lodge and the sphere of light back into your body as before, and close as you usually close a meditation.

Remember that the act of withdrawing the visualized structure into your physical body must never be neglected. Perform this meditation at least four times during the two weeks you spend on this lesson. Eight times is a reasonable maximum.

Tarot Divination

For the next two weeks, continue with the Tarot Divination practice introduced in lesson 15. Try to correlate the cards in the reading with the events of the day, and watch for recurring patterns both in the cards and in the events they reflect. Do this practice each day.

Ritual

Continue to perform the expanded form of the Middle Pillar exercise, with the new final phase given in lesson 15. You may notice changes in this practice developing out of this unit's inner-plane work. In particular, practicing the Middle Pillar exercise in an imagined space may have a variety of effects on the exercise practiced the usual way.

Note in your magical record anything of this sort you may perceive. Pay attention, also, to the differences in feeling and effect between the Middle Pillar exercise done in each of the two ways.

Lesson Review

1. Meditate each day.
2. Perform the daily recollection each day on going to bed (see page 20).
3. Perform the expanded Middle Pillar exercise (see page 234) each day.
4. Perform the Tarot Divination exercise described above each day.

5. Do the course review as described above.
6. Perform the secrecy exercise as described above.
7. Perform the will exercise as described above.
8. Perform the inner-plane working as described above between four and eight times.
9. Keep a record of your work.

When you have spent at least two weeks on these exercises, and done at least the minimum required work, you are ready to proceed to lesson 18, the final lesson of this course.

LESSON 18

THE WAY OF INITIATION

This lesson marks the conclusion of this course and the closing of a phase in your magical studies. In the pages that follow, we have two major goals: to finish our discussion of certain themes that have appeared earlier in this course, and to provide some grounding in what is ahead for those who wish to proceed further along the path of high magic.

Ultimately, these two goals are one and the same, because the further levels of magical study and practice are simply ways of pursuing the same ends discussed already, with the aid of progressively subtler and more powerful techniques and energies.

The most important difference between the material covered in this course and the work taught at more advanced levels has already been discussed: the inclusion of group workings, in which the efforts of a number of trained magicians can be directed toward a single end. Here as elsewhere, from the perspective of the Western esoteric tradition, the most important such end is the process of personal transformation. The generic term for workings that have this purpose is initiation.

initiation

There has probably been more nonsense written about the topic of initiation than about anything else in the Western esoteric tradition, with the possible exception of the lost continent of Atlantis. Much of this nonsense presents initiation as a veiled, mysterious thing, presided over by vast powers and secret chiefs and granting powers that belong in a comic book. On the other hand, there is a substantial amount of nonsense dedicated to the opposite view—that every initiation is a farce, a hoax, or a fraud, a mummery designed to conceal the fact that any real inner development is a matter of personal work and that alone.

As usual, the balanced view lies somewhere between the extremes. An initiation, in the way this term is used by the Western esoteric tradition, is a ritual working designed to do certain specific things:

1. It forms a link between the awareness of the initiate and a transpersonal energy—either the collective energy of a group, or the energy of a deity or spiritual principle invoked and brought into focus by the initiators.
2. It establishes certain symbols in the awareness of the initiate that serve as "handles" for the energy link.
3. It provides the initiate with a set of methods for using these "handles" in individual work, so that energy brought through the link can be brought to bear in specific ways on the task of personal transformation.

One effect of initiation is thus an increase in the amount of force available for individual work. This point is critical: initiation does not replace solitary work; rather, it requires solitary work in order for its potential to be realized. The same is true of any form of group working, from the simplest to the most complex and powerful. Involvement in an initiatory order thus involves daily practices of the sort you've experienced in this course, but focused at least in part on the development of the potential inherent in the group work of the order.

How does initiation function in practical terms? It would be inappropriate to give too many details of the initiations used in any particular magical order, for the simple reason that a certain level of surprise plays an important role in any initiation's psychological effect. Still, we can give a general outline, one that is true for most of the initiatory rites practiced by traditional Western magical groups.

In general terms, candidates for initiation are placed in a heightened state of awareness by certain simple and noninvasive means, and brought into a specially prepared space. In this space, they take an obligation, binding themselves to follow certain rules of conduct as members of the group. Then they move through a set of experiences in which the symbols of the initiation are presented in dramatic form. The candidates then receive the keys that allow access to certain aspects of the initiation's energies, and are formally welcomed into the group as initiates. Throughout the process, their own awareness interacts at several levels with that of the group, as well as with the invoked energies of the initiation. These interactions energize the symbols and keys presented, making them usable by the initiates in personal and group work alike.

Note that at no time in a traditional magical initiation is the initiate hurt or humiliated, nor is any form of force or coercion used. Such things are useless for the purposes of initiatory work, and do not belong in a magical lodge under any circumstances whatever.

The actual effects of an initiation are often subtle, and may not be apparent until after a certain amount of time and further work. It sometimes happens that candidates who have reached a crisis point in their own inner progress may find that an initiatory ritual catalyzes dramatic changes. This is fairly rare. More often, the real results can be seen clearly only in hindsight.

These results are, nonetheless, definite and make the initiatory process one of the central parts of most traditionally oriented magical groups in the Western world. Even the watered-down version of the process practiced by fraternal groups such as the Freemasons and Odd Fellows have kept enough effectiveness to give these groups a surprising longevity and influence.

It is, finally, worth noting that initiation does not absolutely require the presence of a group—or of anyone else besides the initiate. There are rituals of initiation with two participants, an initiator and an initiate; there are also rituals of self-initiation. These last differ noticeably from the lodge initiation format just described, as many of the technical devices of lodge work are usually left out. Self-initiation is generally a less intensive experience than a properly performed lodge initiation. However, it is still a valid way of working, and has a definite place when a novice magician either cannot or does not choose to affiliate with a magical lodge. For this reason, a ritual of self-initiation is included in appendix A.

ENTERING A MAGICAL ORDER

The process of initiation also has another function in most traditional Western magical lodges. It is by way of a ceremony of initiation that new members are brought into the group.

This is more than a mere formality. Every group, from a magical lodge to a sewing circle, has its own personality and energy. Both of these develop out of the personalities and energies of the individuals who make up the group, but both quickly take on characteristics of their own. In a group that has been together for some time, these collective functions help keep the group moving in the direction of its goals, and also produce the almost physical sense of boundary that separates group members from "outsiders."

In the Western esoteric tradition, this aspect of a group is called an *egregor*. Many aspects of group work deal explicitly with the energy and personality of the group egregor, making conscious use of what (outside the magical tradition) is usually an unconscious phenomenon. In a well-run magical order, the group egregor is a major tool of esoteric work, flexible enough to accommodate new members easily, but strong enough to keep the order oriented in the direction of its ideals.

In most traditional magical orders, the link established in the lower grades of initiation is specifically a link with the egregor of the order. Initiates can thus draw on the collective energies of the order in their individual work, and also assist with the renewal and transmission of those energies in group rituals.

A link of this sort carries with it certain consequences. It entails responsibilities on the part of each member to the group, and on the part of the group to each member. Those responsibilities are formalized in the obligation taken during the initiation ceremony, but their essence is simple good faith: a willingness to keep agreements once made, to deal honestly with other group members, to respect the formal structures of the group, and to work together with others toward the achievement of the group's goals.

It's important to recognize, however, that the link is not necessarily permanent. Formed through ritual, it can be broken through ritual as well. In cases when the obligations of membership have been broken by a member, it can be severed by the order. It can also be severed by individual members if they choose to leave the order permanently.

COURSE REVIEW

The last two lessons gave you two different exercises for looking back over the work you've done. Your reactions to the lessons have doubtless taught you certain things; your reactions to your own magical record have taught you others.

Your task now is to synthesize these lessons learned, along with your memories, your opinions, your original hopes and expectations, and your current outlook on the course and its subject, into a general response to the nine months' study and practice you're now finishing.

For you, the value of such a response is significant. As teachers of magic, it's our experience that people come to a course of this kind with a wide range of expectations and an even wider range of motives. In many cases, these expectations and motives may not have been clearly understood, or even conscious. In considering the course, in comparing what you wanted from it with what you got (or didn't get), you may find your own approach to the subject becoming a little clearer. This not only represents a gain in self-knowledge, it also offers the hope that your future esoteric studies will fit your own personal talents and needs more closely.

Over the next two weeks, review your experiences in this course and come to a detailed assessment of the time you've spent with it. Write this out in full and put it away for a week or so, then read it over again and amend it as necessary.

MEDITATION

During the two weeks you spend on this final lesson, continue with the method of discursive meditation presented in lesson 16. As before, your course review and your magical studies will provide you with topics for meditation.

Even after you finish this course and go on to other studies, you are likely to find much value in the habit of meditating each day. While some of the benefits of meditative practice may have become apparent to you during the last nine months, there are aspects to meditation that require years of steady, patient practice to unfold. As with so much of magic, meditation yields its highest potentials over the course of a lifetime's work.

INNER-PLANE WORKING

The last two lessons also gave you a set of inner-plane exercises that work on the interface between ritual and meditative modes of magic. With this final lesson, the development of that interface comes to completion. The practice given here opens up onto almost unlimited possibilities for further work, possibilities that can be pursued either with or apart from a magical lodge.

Your inner-plane work for the next two weeks is identical to the exercises given in lesson 17 except for one change: you will act in your physical and visualized bodies at the same time. This is an essential (to some extent, *the* essential) skill of ritual magic.

1. Begin the practice as before, with the gesture of opening and a banishing ritual, followed by the normal opening for meditation. Project the sphere of golden light from your solar

plexus, followed by the lodge room. Visualize this in as much clarity and solidity as you can manage.

2. When you rise from your chair to begin the active phase of the work, do so physically at the same time as you visualize the action. Unless you have a large practice space, you'll need to treat the chair as the altar on the physical level.

3. Move your physical body around to the back of the chair, to the position in which you did your initial banishing, while you visualize yourself advancing to the altar. (You should not let your visualized and physical bodies separate in space during this process. The trick to doing this is to allow the visualized room to "slide" relative to the physical one, so that the visualized chair in which you were sitting ends up as far behind your position as the altar was originally in front.)

4. Moving in physical and visualized space at the same time, perform the invoking ritual, speaking and vibrating aloud. You will have to open your eyes at intervals in order to move safely (if, in fact, you usually visualize with closed eyes—not everyone does). Try to retain the visualized lodge around you even when your eyes are open.

For the first two sessions you devote to this exercise, follow this practice with the complete Middle Pillar exercise in your joined physical and visualized bodies, and then banish in both bodies, return to the chair, and close as before.

For the second week, provide yourself with a goblet or chalice half full of water—a wine glass will do. If you have a large practice space, place this on a small table, upended box, or other altar substitute that can serve as the physical representation of the visualized altar. If space is cramped, set the goblet under the chair where you will be sitting. (Be careful not to kick it over accidentally!) When you rise from the chair, take a moment to place it in a stable position on the seat before you go behind the chair.

5. Proceed as before, in both bodies, and at the end of the invoking ritual, call down the light as you did in the meditation from last lesson's work.
6. Raise your arms and head, physically as well as in visualization, and build the image of the descending light as clearly and strongly as possible, making sure that the visualized goblet and the real one occupy the same space and receive the same visualized light during this process.
7. Lift both goblets together and drink.
8. Finish by returning to the chair, being careful not to sit on the physical goblet.
9. Close in the same form as before. Once again, always be sure to withdraw the visualized lodge room and the sphere of light back into your body at the end of the practice.

It's possible that this practice may set off certain energy-body reactions that, although not harmful, can be somewhat unnerving. These include:

- dizziness, light-headedness, or vertigo
- a "floating" feeling
- flashes of intense, unexpected imagery
- difficulty concentrating or thinking

If, after you finish one of these meditations, you find yourself experiencing any of these symptoms, eat a large meal as soon as possible. Food in your stomach will ground you and help your energies return to a more balanced state. If possible, let at least six hours pass before doing any other magical work, and avoid alcohol or other mind-altering substances completely during that time. These reactions are an occasional side effect of magical work at an unfamiliar level of intensity, and will go away as you gain experience.

Plan on doing this practice at least four times during the two weeks you devote to this lesson. As before, a total of eight repetitions is probably a sensible maximum for most students.

TAROT DIVINATION

Your tarot work during the next two weeks is the daily tarot divination introduced in lesson 15. With six weeks of practice behind you, you may be able to read the cards well enough to anticipate the way a reading will work out in terms of the day's events. Where it seems appropriate, consider adjusting your choices in accordance with the cards' advice; keep track of the results, as always, in your practice journal.

Like meditation, this is another practice that benefits from patient repetition over months and years. It also serves as an important foundation for the broader study of tarot divination, which you can pursue through books devoted to that subject.

RITUAL

Your ritual work for the next two weeks is the expanded version of the Middle Pillar exercise given in lesson 11, with the final phase from lesson 16 added. It's important that you continue to do this in the ordinary manner, even when you are also doing the first half of this month's meditative work. The two practices have different effects, and draw on different levels of your self. Pay close attention to this difference, and to the effects that each practice seems to have on the other.

The Middle Pillar exercise, like meditation and tarot divination, is something that can be practiced usefully for years. These three basic exercises, performed daily, are the foundation of training in high magic. They make it possible for the magician to make effective use of the more advanced methods of magic.

LESSON REVIEW

1. Perform the meditation each day.
2. Perform the daily recollection each day on going to bed (see page 20).
3. Perform the expanded Middle Pillar exercise as described above each day.
4. Perform the Tarot Divination exercise described above each day.
5. Begin the course review as described in the lesson.
6. Perform the inner-plane working given above at least four times in the two weeks you spend on this lesson.
7. Keep a record of your work.

When you have worked with these exercises for at least two weeks, and have completed at least the minimum required work, you are ready to proceed to the ritual of self-initiation in appendix A.

APPENDIX A

A RITUAL OF SELF-INITIATION

For this ritual, you need your practice space, a chair, and a goblet or wine glass half full of water. Place the goblet under the chair at the opening, unless your practice space is large enough to have an altar or a small table at the center. Use a lit stick of some appropriate incense, such as frankincense, to set the atmosphere, although this is not necessary. You can wear ritual garments such as robes if you so desire.

Read through the ritual carefully before beginning. It is also crucial that you have actually done the work of the course, including but not limited to the inner-plane workings of the last three lessons, before you attempt this ceremony. Self-initiation, like any other kind of initiation, requires some mastery of the basics of magical practice if it is to become anything more than a formality.

Initiation into a magical lodge may come at the beginning of your elementary studies, since presumably the initiators have already done the same work and do much of the work of the initiation. It is true that a very effective self-initiation can be done by a complete novice who blindly takes an oath and then firmly adheres to it despite all pressures to do otherwise. It is also true that you can begin a long self-initiatory process, of the sort presented in medieval magical traditions such as the Abra-Melin work, starting from a state of complete naiveté. However, the effectiveness of a rite of self-initiation has a great deal to do with the preparatory work you put into it.

1. Begin as you did in the inner-plane workings (see page 255), with the gesture of opening and a banishing ritual, followed by the normal opening for meditation. Project the sphere of golden light from your solar plexus, followed by the lodge room; visualize this in as much clarity and solidity as you can manage.

2. Rise from your chair to begin the active phase of the work in both realms, the physical room as well as the visualized one. Perform the Lesser Invoking Ritual of the Pentagram, speaking and vibrating aloud. Visualize the archangels on their thrones as clearly as possible. Then perform the complete Middle Pillar exercise (see page 234) in your joined physical and visualized bodies, standing behind the chair facing east.

3. Take up the goblet in both hands and go physically and in imagination to the east. See yourself standing before the archangel of air in the east. He is seated on his throne, clad in robes of yellow and purple, a sword in his hand. Say aloud:

   Raphael, archangel and guardian of the east, may I partake of the mysteries of air. May the blessing of your element descend upon this water in the name YHVH. (The name is pronounced "Yeh-ho-wah" and should be vibrated.)

4. Pause, and then go to the archangel of fire in the south, clad in red and green and holding a staff. Say aloud:

Michael, archangel and guardian of the south, may I partake of the mysteries of fire. May the blessing of your element descend upon this water in the name ALHIM. (This name is pronounced "Ell-oh-heem" and should be vibrated.)

5. Pause, and then go to the archangel of water in the west, clad in blue and orange and holding a cup. Say aloud:

   Gabriel, archangel and guardian of the west, may I partake of the mysteries of water. May the blessing of your element descend upon this water in the name AL. (This name is pronounced "Ell" and should be vibrated.)

6. Pause, and then go to the archangel of earth in the north, clad in black and earth colors, and holding a pentacle. Say aloud:

   Auriel, archangel and guardian of the north, may I partake of the mysteries of earth. May the blessing of your element descend upon this water in the name ADNI. (This name is pronounced "Ah-doh-nye" and should be vibrated.)

7. Go around to the east again, and then return to the west side of the chair (or your altar), facing east. Say the following aloud:

   I desire to know in order to serve. May the powers of air, of fire, of water, and of earth protect, guide, and illuminate me in my journey on the path of high magic.

8. Raise the goblet (both physical and visualized) in both hands, visualizing light streaming through the skylight at the center of the lodge ceiling. Say aloud:

Come in the power of the Light;
Come in the Light of Wisdom;
Come in the mercy of the Light;
The Light hath healing in its wings!

9. Build the image of the descending light as clearly and strongly as you can, making sure that the visualized goblet and the real one occupy the same space and receive the same visualized light as intensely as possible during this process. Then bring the goblet to your lips and drink. Say aloud:

I accept with thanks the blessings of the elements. I hereby undertake to be as prompt and active as the sylphs, the spirits of air, but avoid frivolity and caprice. I hereby undertake to be as energetic and strong as the salamanders, the spirits of fire, but avoid irritability and ferocity. I hereby undertake to be as flexible and attentive to images as the undines, the spirits of water, but avoid idleness and changeability. I hereby undertake to be as laborious and patient as the gnomes, the spirits of earth, but avoid grossness and avarice. For thus shall I develop the powers of my soul, and fit myself to command the spirits of the elements.

10. Finish by returning to the chair, being careful not to sit on the physical goblet. Close in the usual form as before. Once again, be sure to withdraw the visualized lodge room and the sphere of light back into your body at the end of the practice. As always, note down the working and your experiences in your magical journal.

BIBLIOGRAPHY

Ashcroft-Nowicki, Dolores. *The Ritual Magic Workbook*. York Beach, ME: Weiser, 1998.

Bardon, Franz. *Initiation into Hermetics*. Kettig uber Koblenz: Osiris-Verlag, 1962.

———. *The Key to the True Quabbalah*. Wuppertal: Dieter Ruggeberg, 1971.

———. *The Practice of Magical Evocation*. Graz: Rudolf Pravica, 1967.

Butler, W. E. *Apprenticed to Magic*. Wellingborough, UK: Aquarian, 1962.

———. *How to Read the Aura and Practice Psychometry, Telepathy, and Clairvoyance*. Rochester, VT: Destiny, 1987.

———. *Lords of Light*. Rochester, VT: Destiny, 1990.

———. *The Magician: His Training and Work*. No. Hollywood, CA: Wilshire, 1959.

Cicero, Chic, and Sandra Tabatha Cicero. *Secrets of a Golden Dawn Temple*. St. Paul, MN: Llewellyn, 1992.

Crowley, Aleister. *Book Four*. York Beach, ME: Weiser, 1980.

———. *The Book of Thoth*. York Beach, ME: Weiser, 1969.

———. *Eight Lectures on Yoga*. Scottsdale, AZ: New Falcon, 1991.

———. *Magick in Theory and Practice*. New York: Dover, 1976.

———. *777 and other Qabalistic Writings of Aleister Crowley*. York Beach, ME: Weiser, 1973.

Fortune, Dion. *Applied Magic and Aspects of Occultism*. Wellingborough, UK: Aquarian, 1987.

———. *The Cosmic Doctrine*. York Beach, ME: Weiser, 2000.

———. *Esoteric Orders and Their Work and the Training and Work of the Initiate*. Wellingborough, UK: Aquarian, 1987.

———. *The Magical Battle of Britain*. Bath, UK: Golden Gates, 1993.

———. *The Mystical Qabalah*. York Beach, ME: Weiser, 1984.

———. *Psychic Self-Defence*. London: Rider, 1930.

Fortune, Dion, and Gareth Knight. *An Introduction to Ritual Magic*. Loughborough, UK: Thoth, 1997.

———. *The Circuit of Force*. Loughborough, UK: Thoth, 1998.

Gardner, Adelaide. *Meditation: A Practical Study*. Wheaton, IL: TPH, 1968.

Godwin, David. *Godwin's Cabalistic Encyclopedia*. St. Paul, MN: Llewellyn, 1989.

Gray, William G. *Concepts of Qabalah*. York Beach, ME: Weiser, 1984.

———. *Sangreal Ceremonies and Rituals*. York Beach, ME: Weiser, 1985.

———. *The Sangreal Sacrament*. York Beach, ME: Weiser, 1983.

———. *Western Inner Workings*. York Beach, ME: Weiser, 1982.

Greer, John Michael. *Circles of Power: Ritual Magic in the Western Tradition*. St. Paul, MN: Llewellyn, 1997.

——. *Earth Divination, Earth Magic*. St. Paul, MN: Llewellyn, 1999.

——. *Monsters*. St. Paul, MN: Llewellyn, 2001.

——. *Natural Magic*. St. Paul, MN: Llewellyn, 2000.

——. *Paths of Wisdom: The Magical Cabala in the Western Tradition*. St. Paul, MN: Llewellyn, 1996.

Haddock, Frank Channing. *Power of Will*. Meriden, CT: Pelton, 1918.

Hall, Manly Palmer. *Self-Unfoldment through Disciplines of Realization*. Los Angeles, CA: PRS, 1946.

Hulse, David Allen. *New Dimensions for the Cube of Space*. York Beach, ME: Weiser, 2000.

Knight, Gareth. *A Practical Guide to Qabalistic Symbolism*. York Beach, ME: Weiser, 1978.

——. *Magical Images and the Magical Imagination*. Albuquerque, NM: Sun Chalice, 1998.

——. *Occult Exercises and Practices*. Albuquerque, NM: Sun Chalice, 1997.

——. *The Practice of Ritual Magic*. Albuquerque, NM: Sun Chalice, 1996.

——. *The Secret Tradition in Arthurian Legend*. Wellingborough, UK: Aquarian, 1983.

Lawlor, Robert. *Sacred Geometry: Philosophy and Practice*. New York: Thames & Hudson, 1982.

Levi, Eliphas. *Transcendental Magic*, tr. Arthur Edward Waite. York Beach, ME: Weiser, 1972.

Lomer, Georg. *Seven Hermetic Letters*, tr. Gerhard Hanswille and Franca Gallo. Salt Lake City, UT: Merkur, 1997.

Regardie, Israel. *Ceremonial Magic*. Wellingborough, UK: Aquarian, 1980.

———. *Foundations of Practical Magic*. Wellingborough, UK: Aquarian, 1979.

———. *The Golden Dawn*. St. Paul, MN: Llewellyn 1971.

———. *The Middle Pillar*. St. Paul, MN: Llewellyn, 1970.

Sadhu, Mouni. *Concentration*. No. Hollywood, CA: Wilshire, 1959.

———. *Meditation*. No. Hollywood, CA: Wilshire, 1967.

———. *The Tarot*. No. Hollywood, CA: Wilshire, 1962.

Steiner, Rudolf. *A Way of Self-Knowledge*. Hudson, NY: Anthroposophic Press, 1999.

———. *How to Know Higher Worlds*. Hudson, NY: Anthroposophic Press, 1994.

"Three Initiates." *The Kybalion*. Chicago, IL: Yogi Pub. Society, 1912.

Wang, Robert. *The Secret Temple*. New York: Weiser, 1980.

Waterfield, Robin, trans. *The Theology of Arithmetic*. Grand Rapids, MI: Phanes, 1988.

Yates, Frances. *The Art of Memory*. Chicago, IL: University of Chicago Press, 1966.

INDEX

TO OUR READERS

Weiser Books, an imprint of Red Wheel/Weiser, publishes books across the entire spectrum of occult and esoteric subjects. Our mission is to publish quality books that will make a difference in people's lives without advocating any one particular path or field of study. We value the integrity, originality, and depth of knowledge of our authors.

Our readers are our most important resource, and we appreciate your input, suggestions, and ideas about what you would like to see published. Please feel free to contact us, to request our latest book catalog, or to be added to our mailing list.

Red Wheel/Weiser, LLC
665 Third Street, Suite 400
San Francisco, CA 94107
www.redwheelweiser.com